Inclusive Schools, Inclusive Society

race and identity on the agenda

Produced by
Race On The Agenda
in partnership with
Association of London Government and
Save the Children

Written and compiled for Race On The Agenda
by Robin Richardson and Angela Wood, Insted consultancy

Published by
Trentham Books

First published in 1999 by Trentham Books Limited

Reprinted 2000

Trentham Books Limited
Westview House
734 London Road
Oakhill
Stoke on Trent
Staffordshire
England ST4 5NP

British Cataloguing in Publication Data
A catalogue record for this book is available from the British Library
ISBN: 1 85856 203 1

Designed and typeset by Trentham Print Design Ltd., Chester
and printed in Great Britain by Bemrose Shafron (Printers) Ltd., Chester.

CONTENTS

Acknowledgements

Background

This book is published by Trentham for Race On The Agenda (ROTA), in partnership with the Association of London Government (ALG) and Save the Children Fund (SCF).

ROTA is a policy development, information and research service for London's Black and Minority Ethnic voluntary sector. It is funded by London Boroughs Grants and the National Lottery Charities Board.

Save the Children is the UK's leading international children's charity. It works in more than 65 countries, including the UK, championing the right of children to a happy, healthy and secure childhood.

The Association of London Government represents London's 32 boroughs and the Corporation of London.

Steering committee

The compilation of the book was supervised by a steering committee whose members were Marina Ahmad (ROTA), Rosalind Hardie (ALG), Dharmendra Kanani (ROTA – chair), Brian Richardson (ROTA), Nicky Road (SCF) and Claudia Smith (ALG).

Compilation and editorial

The book was compiled and written by Robin Richardson and Angela Wood, directors of the Insted educational consultancy.

Background research

The book draws on recent research findings by Maud Blair and Jill Bourne (Open University for the Department for Education and Employment), David Gillborn and Caroline Gipps (University of London), Audrey Osler (University of Birmingham for the Commission for Racial Equality), Tony Sewell (University of Leeds) and Debbie Weekes and Cecile Wright (Nottingham Trent University for the Runnymede Trust). There are full bibliographical references on page 85. In addition the book draws at one stage on research summaries made by the London Research Centre and the Social Exclusion Unit, details on page 84. Further, the book takes into account recent findings by the Office for Standards in Education (Ofsted), published in *Raising the Attainment of Minority Ethnic Pupils*, March 1999.

Local authorities

Assistance in the compilation of this book was given by officers, inspectors and teachers in several London authorities, including Brent, Camden, Croydon, Ealing, Enfield, Greenwich, Hammersmith and Fulham, Haringey, Harrow, Hounslow, Islington, Lambeth, Lewisham, Newham, Sutton, Tower Hamlets, Waltham Forest, Wandsworth and Westminster. The book also draws on reports and documents from Birmingham, Bradford, Leicester, Slough and Staffordshire.

Organisations

Acknowledgement is made to Camden Racial Equality Council for the involvement of the director, Dharmendra Kanani, and for providing accommodation for meetings.

The book draws on information and advice from the Working Group Against Racism in Children's Resources (WGARCR), Lady Margaret Hall. 460 Wandsworth Road, London SW8 3LX.

Individuals

Assistance was given by Eileen Arnold, Karen Badgery, Maud Blair, Teresa Clark, Sue Clarke, Kate Daly, Chris Geohagen, Gerry German, David Gillborn, Jackie Harrop, Gerry Hicken, Jennifer James, Celestine Keise, Kathy Maclean, Fahro Malik, Berenice Miles, Judith March, Michael Marland, James Morrison, Audrey Osler, Paul Roper, Beverley Ruddock, Easter Russell, Amer Saad, Graham Smith, Jayant Tanna and Michael Vance.

Quotations

Acknowledgement is made to the following: Harrap for the extract from a poem by James Berry (page 2); Faber for the quotation from *Skylight* by David Hare (page 3); David Fulton for the extract from *Race Relations in the Primary School* by Cecile Wright (page 4), Department for Education and Employment for the summary (page 14) and the quotations (pages 53 and 58) from *Making the Difference* by Maud Blair and Jill Bourne; Picador for the extracts from *Trumpet* by Jackie Kay (page 18, 19); Jonathan Cape, for the extract from *East, West* by Salman Rushdie (page 21); ARC Theatre Publications for the quotation from *Ooh Ah Showab Khan* (page 23); Faber for quotations from *The Buddha of Suburbia* (page 26) and *The Black Album* (page 31) by Hanif Kureishi; Runnymede Trust for material developed from *This is Where I Live* (page 6-7), *Islamophobia: a challenge to us all* (page 22) and *Equality Assurance in Schools* (pages 25 and 40); Greenwich Council for material from *Routes of Racism* (page 23); Trentham Books, for material from *Enriching Literacy* by Brent Language Service (pages 44-47).

Publisher and design

Acknowledgement is due to Trentham Books and Trentham Print Design for their partnership, advice and assistance in matters of design, printing, publishing and distribution. The cover design is by Shawn Stipling of Aquarium Graphic Design.

FOREWORD

The time is right for change, don't let this opportunity pass you by, cling to it with both hands.

For a long time, I have talked about education as the key to children's development. The curriculum that is taught in schools needs to incorporate each individual child's background, to give them self-worth and for them to have pride in who they are.

Black history classes are important for all of us. It is our different backgrounds that separate us and by bringing children together in the classroom, we lay the foundations for a better future for all children in the country.

By taking up the challenge, we as adults have the responsibility to ensure that we don't fail our children by denying them the right to gain in all aspects of learning. This is what education is all about.

Doreen Lawrence

SUMMARY

Background

This book was commissioned and produced by Race On The Agenda (ROTA), in partnership with the Association of London Government (ALG) and Save the Children Fund (SCF). ROTA is a policy development, information and research service for London's Black and Minority Ethnic voluntary sector. It is funded by London Boroughs Grants and the National Lottery Charities Board.

Who is the book for?

- Generally, this book is for everyone interested in raising the achievement of Black and Minority Ethnic young people in schools, with a view to making Britain a fairer and better place – a more inclusive society.

- More specifically, it is for everyone involved in making sure that the new Ethnic Minority Achievement Grant, introduced by the government in 1999, is well used by schools and local authorities in the years ahead.

- So the book is for:

  - senior staff in schools, particularly headteachers

  - classroom teachers

  - members of governing bodies

  - local authority officers, inspectors and elected members

  - parents

  - members of community groups and organisations.

Is the book for all phases of education, including nursery, primary, special and secondary?

Yes, the book as a whole is intended for all phases. As much of it as possible is generic in its terminology, references and assumptions, rather than phase-specific. Inevitably, however, certain parts of the book may appear geared more to one phase than to others.

What is the book based on?

- A number of recent research and evaluation studies, including work funded and published by the Commission for Racial Equality, the Runnymede Trust and the Department for Education and Employment, and books by individual scholars. There is more information about these in the box on page viii.

- Study of statistics and proposals submitted to the Department for Education and Employment in connection with the Ethnic Minority Achievement Grant.

- Consideration of the observations in the Macpherson Report, *The Stephen Lawrence Inquiry*, about institutional racism in British society, and about implications of the report's recommendations and concepts for the education system.

- Interviews and meetings with a range of people professionally involved in the issues with which the book deals.

- Submissions and papers from individual schools and local authorities.

How is this book different from other books on similar themes?

What makes this book distinctive is that it contains much discussion and training material – many of its pages may be photocopied and used in staff meetings and inservice training, in meetings involving parents and governors, and in meetings in community organisations.

Since the book is intended principally for discussion purposes, its terminology is less academic than the terminology in most other publications on the same topics. Similarly its layout and general appearance are less formal.

Other differences include the fact that the book contains statistics which have not previously been published, and that it contains quotations from fiction and drama, and extracts from the writings of children and young people.

Does the book have a particular geographical focus?

Yes, it derives from concerns in schools and education authorities in greater London, and most of the statistics and examples which it contains have their origins in London. However, there is virtually nothing in the book which distinctively belongs to London. Overall, the book can be used throughout the country.

Schools and teachers are already under much stress. Does this book not add to the stress? And what about resources? What resources, if any, are available for implementing the recommendations outlined in this book?

Certainly, teachers and schools are nowadays under much stress. But there's no reason why this book should add to it. On the contrary, the book is likely to help schools and teachers cope constructively with the pressures they experience. As for resources, there is now a specific grant, the Ethnic Minority Achievement Grant, which schools can use – though basically the ideas in this book do not need new money. Certainly lack of money cannot be an excuse for failing to provide what the Macpherson report calls 'a professional and appropriate service'.

How is the book to be used?

Essentially the book is a manual for planning and action. It contains reflection and statistics, but also much material for discussion. Many of the pages have been laid out so that they can be conveniently photocopied, and used in meetings and training sessions.

What are the book's principal themes and concerns?

● The book explains and illustrates at length the concept of an 'inclusive school'. The concept refers both to the curriculum and to a school's overall atmosphere and ethos – as it were, a school's 'institutional body language'.

● An inclusive school recognises and respects the cultural and personal identities and life-experiences of its pupils or students, and helps them to develop their personal identities amidst many conflicting pressures. 'Identity' is another of the book's principal concepts.

● An inclusive school recognises that racism, in a range of subtle (and sometimes unsubtle) ways, continues to blight the lives of large numbers of people in Britain today. The book uses and explains the concept of institutional racism and distinguishes between four main dimensions: (a) exclusion and non-participation (b) discrimination, both direct and indirect (c) violence and harassment (d) prejudice and hostility in attitudes, assumptions and organisational cultures.

● An inclusive school teaches an inclusive curriculum and develops and maintains an inclusive ethos. Within this policy context, it deliberately and explicitly resolves to cut down on its use of permanent and fixed-term exclusions and to ensure that there are no differentials in the exclusion rates of pupils and students from different ethnic backgrounds.

What will be achieved if the book is successful?

All children and young people will benefit. Inclusive schools are good places for all children and young people to be. An inclusive society benefits all people who live in it.

Within this context of benefits for all, there will be fewer exclusions from schools of Black and other minority pupils and the educational achievement of Black and other minority pupils will be higher.

BACKGROUND RESEARCH

This book draws on findings, views and recommendations in:

Black Masculinities and Schooling: how Black boys survive modern schooling by Tony Sewell, Trentham Books 1997.

Exclusion from School and Racial Equality: a good practice guide, based on a research report by Audrey Osler (University of Birmingham), Commission for Racial Equality, 1998.

Improving Practice: a whole school approach to raising the achievement of African Caribbean youth, by Debbie Weekes and Cecile Wright (Nottingham Trent University), Runnymede Trust, 1998.

Making the Difference: teaching and learning strategies in successful multi-ethnic schools, by Maud Blair and Jill Bourne et al (Open University), Department for Education and Employment.

Raising the Attainment of Minority Ethnic Pupils: school and LEA responses, Office for Standards in Education, 1999.

This is Where I Live: stories and pressures in Brixton, Runnymede Trust 1996.

INDEX TO BOXES

Examples, stories and quotations

The book contains many examples and quotations. Most of these are presented in boxes separate from the main text. They are as follows:

Sources

Where material in a box is derived from another publication, the source is acknowledged in the box itself. If there is no acknowledgement, the material was created especially for this book. For many of the boxes there are background notes on page 84.

COMING TO TERMS

What's in word?

'Ethnic minority' or 'minority ethnic' or 'Black'? Are these terms interchangeable or do they have distinctively different meanings or implications? And what about other terms in relation to the subject-matter of this book? For example, 'Caribbean', 'Afro-Caribbean', 'African-Caribbean', 'West Indian'? The word 'race' itself, and the related words 'racial', 'racist' and 'racism'?

A book such as this cannot lay down rulings on the 'correct' meanings and usage of words such as 'Black', 'race', 'ethnicity', and so forth. It can, however, note some of the semantic problems. And it can explain how words are used between its own covers. Hence this page.

Some of the problems

The semantic problems in this field (as also in other fields which involve issues of equality and social justice) include the following:

1   The same word can have different meanings or implications for different people.

2   Words can change in their meanings over time, and in whether or not they give offence.

3   A word may mean one thing to academics and other specialists and rather different things in the media and popular usage. (For example, notoriously, the word 'ethnic'.)

4   A word or phrase often belongs to a body of discourse and tradition, so that in using it one may be showing or implying (though perhaps without realising this) where one stands on broad political, historical and ideological issues.

5   Reality itself is continually changing, as also are ways people define their own identity, and language cannot easily keep up. Also, people continually need new words to articulate new insights and understandings.

6   Semantic disputes are often connected to disputes about values. What are the problems we are seeking to address? How shall we approach them? What sort of society do we want to create and protect?

This book

In this book choices about specific words and terms have been made in the context of the three key ideas in the book's title – inclusiveness, race and identity. In particular the key concepts of race and racism, as discussed at length in Chapter 3, are centrally relevant.

'Black'

The word Black (with a capital letter) is used throughout this book to refer to people targeted by racism, and to recall continually that race and racism are fundamental issues. To omit the word Black here (and to use, for example, a term such as 'ethnic minority' or 'minority ethnic' instead), would be to gloss over the realities of racism, and would in this way make the realities more difficult to address.

Also, the word Black is the preferred way which many people adopt – people of South Asian origin as well as African or Caribbean origin – to define their own identity, and to summarise the experiences, struggles and objectives which they have in common. For this reason too, the word Black is used throughout this book.

The complexity of racism

Racism takes a range of different forms – so much so that some people speak and write of racisms rather than racism, to stress the variety of forms. Using the term Black to refer to all people who experience racism may therefore risk obscuring significant realities, particularly the forms and strands of racism which use cultural or religious identity as markers of difference rather than, or as well as, physical markers. For example, it may obscure forms of hostility and hatred such as Islamophobia (irrational hatred or fear of Islam) and antisemitism. People targeted by Islamophobia define their identity as Muslim, primarily, not as Black.

Inclusive vocabulary

A book on inclusiveness should itself attempt to be inclusive or comprehensive in its use of language, so that people engaging with it do not feel disregarded, excluded, alienated or invisible. For this reason the adjectival term 'Black and other minority' is sometimes used in this book rather than 'Black' on its own, in order to recall racism's differences in form.

The book does not use the terms 'ethnic minority' or 'minority ethnic' as adjectives, except when quoting directly from other sources. This is because in popular usage the term 'ethnic' is widely misunderstood to be simply a synonym for 'not-white' or 'not-western'.

In references to particular aspects of Black experience, the book throughout uses the term 'African-Caribbean' in preference to 'Afro-Caribbean', 'Black Caribbean' or 'Caribbean Heritage', and uses the term 'South Asian' to refer to people with origins in Bangladesh, India, Pakistan or Sri Lanka.

I. OVERVIEW

In this chapter the concept of inclusiveness, both in schools and in wider society, is introduced and explained. There are references to the everyday life of school classrooms, and to statistics compiled in connection with the Ethnic Minority Achievement Grant. The chapter starts with quotations from a well-known poem by the Caribbean writer James Berry, and continues with stories about two real people, Carl aged seven and Ursula aged 15.

Headings in this chapter

Boxes in this chapter

My teacher's eyes

'I wish ...,' says the child at the start of James Berry's well-known poem *Dreaming Black Boy*. It is an appropriate way to start a poem about education. A quotation from the poem is an appropriate way to introduce the themes and concerns of this book. How does the education system treat Black children and young people? What sort of future for them is being prepared? What hopes do they and their teachers have for a fairer and more inclusive society? These are the principal questions which the poem raises, and which are addressed at length in this book. The opening three stanzas of the poem are quoted in Box 1.

The first wish in the poem is utterly simple: 'I wish my teacher's eyes wouldn't go past me today.' The meaning is both literal and metaphorical. Literally, the boy wants to feel that he is noticed, that his presence is taken account of. Metaphorically, and even more importantly, he wants to be cared about and attended to. It follows that when he does something praiseworthy – when he achieves some worthwhile target – he wants this to be

noticed too, and affirmed: 'I wish he'd know it's okay to hug me when I kick a goal.' It is not empty or ritualistic praise he's asking for, not sweet nothings, but something focused, genuine and spontaneous, and in relation to real achievement.

Body language

Berry stresses that attention and respect are expressed and received (and sometimes of course not expressed, not received) in a range of ways, not by words alone. Tone of voice, facial expression, gesture, posture, demeanour, closeness or distance, the arrangement of objects and furniture, all these affect the messages which human beings give and send to each other, and which they receive.

Also, there is such a thing as 'institutional body language' – messages are given and received through an organisation's customs, procedures, rules, regulations. This is true in schools as everywhere else. The point is obvious and well-known, yet needs stressing.

Particularly the point needs stressing in the schools for which this book is intended, multi-ethnic schools. In such schools much communication – both in words and in body language – is inherently and inescapably cross-cultural, cross-ethnic. For this reason alone there may be misunderstandings and crossed wires. A further complicating factor is inequality, specifically inequality caused or exacerbated by racism. It is particularly within a context of inequality that what is said is not necessarily what is heard.

Box 1

'I wish' – a child dreams

I wish my teacher's eyes wouldn't
go past me today. Wish he'd know
it's okay to hug me when I kick
a goal. Wish I myself wouldn't
hold back when an answer comes.

I wish I could be educated
to the best of tune-up and earn
good money and not sink to lick boots. I wish I could
go on every crisscross way of the globe,
and no persons or powers or
hotel keepers would make it a waste.

I wish life wouldn't spend me out
opposing. Wish same way creation
would have me stand it would have me stretch, and
hold high, my voice Paul Robeson's, my inside eye
a sun.

(From **Dreaming Black Boy**, by James Berry, in
Bluefoot Traveller, Harrap 1981)

Thousands missing out, admits Blunkett

SCHOOLS FAILING BLACK PUPILS

The Express, March 8, 1999

Disposition

'When they approach me they see...everything and anything except me....[this] invisibility...occurs because of a peculiar disposition of the eyes....' Ralph Ellison, *Invisible Man*

OVERVIEW ●

Learning

Berry's next point is about learning, and about the inevitability in all learning of risk-taking. All learning is hazardous, for you have to risk making mistakes, getting it wrong before you get it right. 'I wish I myself wouldn't hold back,' the boy says, 'when an answer comes.'

'An answer comes': a thought, a possible solution to a problem, a possible resolution of an enigma, an anomaly, a puzzle. It comes from within you and you have to test it out by uttering it and this can be scary. But this is what learning and education entail. There is no way forward other than through risks. Again, Berry is saying what everyone knows, but which needs recalling and rehearsing.

The essential task for teachers, it follows, is to provide both security, which comes from attending to and affirming the pupils, and also challenge, in order that they may learn. In David Hare's play *Skylight* a teacher observes that 'education has to be a mixture of haven and challenge'. And she goes on: 'Finding that balance, it stretches you, it stretches you as far as you'll go.' Her words are quoted at fuller length in Box 2.

The goals

Security and challenge are means, not ends: pre-conditions or foundations, not the final goal. The goals, says Berry, are an educated mind and the capacity to take part in society. 'I wish I could be educated to the best of tune-up, and earn good money, and not sink to lick boots.' The boy wants his mind to be like a well-tuned engine or musical instrument.

A specialist term for his wish here is 'cognitive and conceptual development': he wants thinking, reasoning and problem-solving skills, and control of concepts in the main academic disciplines. And at the same time, wholly reasonably, he wants good paper qualifications, leading to a good job and to a respected place in wider society: '... earn good money, and not sink to lick boots'. He wants his contributions to society to be welcome and worthwhile, not wasted: 'I wish I could go every criss-cross way of the globe, and no powers or persons or hotel-keepers would make it a waste'.

Definitely he wants to be part of society, to be able to say 'yes' to it. The contrary, to spend his life saying 'no', would be waste: 'I wish life wouldn't spend me out opposing'.

> *Box 2*
> ## Haven and challenge
> 'Education has to be a mixture of haven and challenge. Reassurance, of course. Stability. But also incentive. At the very least you offer the kids support. You care for them. You offer them security. You give them an environment where they feel they can grow. But also you make bloody sure you challenge them. You make sure they realise learning is hard. Because if you don't, if you only make it a safe haven, if it's all clap-happy and 'everything the kids do is great', then what are you creating? Emotional toffees, who've actually learnt nothing, but who then have to go back and face the real world ... Finding that balance, it stretches you, it stretches you as far as you'll go.'
> *Source: **Skylight** by David Hare, 1995.*

Finally, in this extract from Berry's poem, the boy dreams of his own personal creativity and powers of insight and imagination, and his own unique relationship to the total universe: 'Wish ... creation would have me stand, stretch, hold high, my voice Paul Robeson's, my inside eye a sun'. As he looks to the future, and utters his wishes, the boy is representative of all children in British schools, not of Black children only.

What chance?

What chance does Berry's boy have? What chance that indeed his teacher's eyes will not go past him today? Nor any day, over the years ahead? What chance that he will receive from his teacher today, and from many other teachers in the future, a balance of haven and challenge? What chance of decent qualifications, a decent job, a respected, powerful and contributing place in mainstream society? These are questions which the poem raises. And they are the questions with which this whole book is concerned.

Judging not only by statistics but also by countless impressionistic anecdotes, the future is basically not bright. Consider little Carl, for example, about whom there is a story in Box 3, and Ursula, the teenager who is quoted in Box 4. Carl, it is reasonable to assume, has the same dreams and wishes as James Berry's boy. He too wants to be included. The exact opposite happens to him.

Box 3

Get out of my class! – a case-study in exclusion

A class of 7-8 year-olds settles down to work after morning break. The children are seated four to a table. The classroom noise varies from low to medium level. The teacher, seated at her desk marking children's work, keeps a vigil on a table where four children sit: an African-Caribbean boy (Carl), two White boys and a White girl. Every time the classroom noise level increases, the teacher looks at Carl, who works effortlessly at the task set him, stopping occasionally to converse with the White boys seated at his table.

Teacher: Carl, get on with your work.

Carl gives her a disparaging sideways glance. Attends to his work. The classroom noise decreases temporarily, then rises again. The teacher looks up from her marking and sees that Carl and the White boys at his table are now avoiding the task.

Teacher (*shouting*): Carl, stop disrupting the class!

Carl: It's not only me. (*Points to the others at his table*) They're not working either.

Teacher (*shouting*): Carl, leave my class, go and work outside. I'm not having you disrupting the class.

Carl picks up his book and leaves the room, giving the teacher a disparaging sideways glance as he leaves.

Teacher (*addressing the class*): Look at that face. (*Turning to Carl*) Go on, outside. The trouble with you is that you have a chip on your shoulder.

Carl spends the rest of the day outside the classroom, working in the corridor.

Source: adapted slightly from **Race Relations in the Primary School** by Cecile Wright, 1992

Teachers with attitude

The eyes of Carl's teacher do not go past him today. But she looks at him not in order to recognise, affirm and include, but because she is on her watch against him. Her own view is that Carl has an attitude problem – 'look at that face'. But from Carl's point of view, and from the point of view of anyone reading this book inclined to see the world and its affairs though Carl's eyes, it is the teacher's attitude, not Carl's, that causes the situation to escalate so fast into his being excluded from the room. Carl's problem, it could be said, is 'teachers with attitude'.

This view is elaborated by the teenage Black girl quoted in Box 4. 'I'm sorry,' she says, 'this doesn't sound very nice, but sometimes it's the teachers who set off the children, they talk wicked to the children... They look at you rude'. Her remarks contain many points of interest, including three in particular. First, she does not make a blanket condemnation of all teachers – and nor, incidentally, does this book! On the contrary she goes out of her way to mention and commend teachers who 'talk' to her as distinct from shout or threaten. Second, she does not exonerate herself and her friends. She and they 'get into trouble', she freely admits, and their problems are partly of their own making. From this recognition real and lasting behavioural change could flow, if sympathetic adults, particularly teachers, are present to support and encourage. Third, she poignantly uses the teenage concept of 'respect' to summarise not only what she wants to receive from her peers but also what she needs and desires from her teachers. A view propounded in this book is that that is not, absolutely it is not, too much to ask.

Box 4

Respect – a teenager talking, 1999

Ursula (not her real name) is in Year 10 at a school in London. She has been permanently excluded from two other schools, and also has been subjected to a number of fixed-term and unofficial exclusions since joining her present school. She is a brilliant athlete and singer and is clearly of above average academic ability. She reflects here with a sympathetic teacher about her school career and perceptions. The transcript has been slightly edited to remove identifiable references to other staff.

Ursula: Other schools, like, they didn't really help you, they didn't really talk to children like you do, they just say 'you've got one more chance' and then if you do something you're excluded. They don't talk to you. This school now, they give you chances, they talk to you about it.

Teacher: How can we help people not to be excluded?

Ursula: It's just that, I think that they should have a programme for all the children that get into trouble, that once a week we could talk about it, about problems we're having. We could have our say too, and write about it. Maybe a teacher could be there, but we could share our views, we could talk to each other. If I talk to the right teacher –

Teacher: What else could the school do to help, to try to avoid excluding you? In terms of how we act towards you?

Ursula: I'm sorry, this doesn't sound very nice, but sometimes it's the teachers who set off the children, they talk wicked to the children, they think because they're teachers they can say 'shut up' and 'sit down you stupid girl or boy'. They talk to them like that but it's best to be respectful, it's best –

Teacher: How can we show respect? How should we talk?

Ursula: You say 'can you be quiet?' Then if the person goes on talking you've got a right to say 'shut up', but you don't just say 'shut up' straight away. You just ask them to be quiet. They, they just ... It's how they talk to you, but you should just talk to them naturally, how you talk to the person next to you.

Teacher: Are there other ways, apart from in language?

Ursula: Body language, yeah. Like we see how some of the teachers look at you rude. And if I see a teacher looking at me rude, and she's going to do something, I'm gonna say something, and that's what starts it off. Body language has got to be good as well.

Teacher: Apart from the look on our faces, how could we use body language to show you respect?

Ursula: *Oh, respect?! [The punctuation marks and italics are the teacher's own, as she transcribes the conversation]* Don't point. *(She demonstrates a teacher pointing their finger into someone's face.)* Don't do that.

Teacher: Is respect important?

Ursula: Yeah. The more respect, the better a school gets, cos if the children are happy the school's better, and the more respect the child will have for the teacher.

Teacher: Is there anything else we could do?

Ursula: Well, I just like the idea of the group I told you about, but would it be allowed?

Teacher: Why not?

Ursula: I don't think so ... I can't say nothing. We'll just have to wait and see.

(Source: a school submitting evidence for the production of this book, February 1999)

Box 5

Life and life-chances – a case study in waste

Ages 5 – 8

Some of his teachers expected him to be a troublemaker. Had not the media and history books told them, or subtly suggested to them, that people like him are likely to troublesome, even at the age of five? Was this assumption not in the very air they breathed?

Not that they were consciously aware that they had been affected by media imagery, or by a legacy of negative stereotypes, or by the cultural contexts in which they daily moved and talked. But all the same they criticised and checked him more than they did other children, and more than was necessary. They had, they thought, to keep him under tight control.

Ages 8 – 11

It slowly became clear to him, though he couldn't himself have yet voiced it like this, that he had a choice. Either he could accept the teachers' valuations of himself, as an object to be feared and controlled, or – with a sense of mounting injustice – he could resist, could assert himself, stand up for himself. He chose the latter.

To begin with, his assertiveness took the form of ignoring instructions, or complying with them only slowly. Later, it took the form of questioning, asking for reasons, challenging, disobeying. The teachers' expectations, as they saw the matter, were confirmed: indeed, he was an aggressive troublemaker, he had attitude, he was someone to be kept under tight control if at all possible.

One result of these tensions and conflicts was that he became increasingly less interested in the whole business of writing. Since no one was interested in what he said or thought, why should he bother to write? He was not only a troublemaker, his teachers could see, but not at all bright either.

Ages 11 – 15

To begin with, at secondary school, he was happy. He felt that whatever had been wrong at primary school was now behind him. But within only a few weeks things began to go wrong again. There was that day a teacher said something slightly sarcastic about him, and other kids laughed. The day he was beaten in a playground fight. The day he was badly let down by his own poor writing skills. Embarrassed about his poor writing skills, he avoided writing as much as he could.

He began to suspect – though still he could not have voiced this – that the school didn't care about him, for it didn't recognise and include him, it didn't seem to know him. Also, to his dismay, he found that his parents were unwilling or unable to help him. They too didn't seem to understand what he was going through.

He did, however, feel recognition, inclusion and respect from his friends. It was his friends who made coming to school each day worthwhile. Unfortunately, these friends were every bit as disenchanted with the official school system as he was himself. They too found writing a tedious chore. They too were seen as troublemakers. For they too questioned, challenged, didn't take kindly to being given instructions and orders. They too believed that the school was frequently unfair. And they too were influenced, as he was, by young people a few years older than themselves, anti-school, anti-police, anti-authority.

Troubles and tensions mounted. Getting involved in fights and needing, he strongly believed, to prove his manhood by being hard, being bad – he must have respect from his peers or life wouldn't be worth living. Being thrown out of lessons. Detentions. Letters home from the school. Formal warnings. Various fixed-term exclusions. Eventually, he was permanently excluded from his school.

Ages 15 – 18

He didn't settle at his new secondary school. He was entered for a full range of GCSEs, but missed most of the exams. He left school with minimal, indeed worthless, paper qualifications. No chance of employment. He wasn't interested in training, since so far as he could see there weren't any jobs available any way. Drifted, along with his friends, into drugs and crime. Frequently stopped by the police. Eventually, convictions and detention. I don't care, he said, whether I live or die, and I don't care whether anyone else does, either.

(Source: based on work in Lambeth schools and youth service, and developed from material in *This Is Where I Live: stories and pressures in Brixton*, published by the Runnymede Trust, 1995.)

Life and life-chances

This book is concerned with both specifics and generalities, both tiny details and broad pictures – Berry's boy, Hare's teacher, Carl, Ursula on the one hand, and – for example – statistics and the Ethnic Minority Achievement Grant on the other.

One way of holding the two poles together is through the device of a fable or cautionary tale, for example the story 'Life and life-chances' which appears in Box 5. At first sight, such a story is about one specific person. In fact, however, it has been crafted to encode a range of general ideas, arguments and proposals. It was created as discussion material for teachers and youth workers and has also been used with parents. Is the story recognisably about people we know, and about events and processes with which we are familiar? What is it saying about them? Do we agree with what it is saying? What does it leave it out? Is it unacceptably biased? What are, or may be, the practical implications? These are some of the questions which the story raises. In Box 6, entitled 'If?', there are some reflections about the story's practical implications.

Research and statistics

For the launch of the Ethnic Minority Achievement Grant, from April 1999 onwards, the government required all local authorities to submit statistics relating to achievement by ethnicity at Key Stage 2 and in GCSE in summer 1998. For the compilation of this book, a number of authorities in or near London were invited to share the figures which they had collected. In the following pages there are notes on the principal findings. The authorities are given fictitious names, to avoid invidious or misleading comparisons. There is first a note about terminology.

Box 6

If – reflections on a life

(*To be read in conjunction with Box 5, 'Life and life-chances – a case study in waste'.*)

If more of his teachers had resisted media imagery and the legacy of history, both as individuals and collectively, as a staffroom and as a profession.

If more of the staff had seen and treated him as an individual.

If they had taken a sympathetic interest in who he was, and in his family and community stories, and in the future ahead of him. If they had been able to tell him and show him that they had high hopes for him.

If more of the teachers had looked at themselves and their own attitudes and ways of interacting with pupils. If they had given him a sense that they respected him and had high expectations of him.

If the school had provided a curriculum which recognised and included his identity, history and future.

If the staff had been able to help him develop skills in avoiding destructive conflicts with themselves.

If his parents and family friends had realised what was happening, and had spoken up for him.

If a friendly adult had helped him to identify the extent to which he was himself contributing to his problems, and could himself do something to solve them.

If there had been sympathetic adults around, both at school and at a youth club or centre, who could have seen at an early stage what was happening, and could have worked with him and his friends – mediating in conflicts, advocating and defending where necessary, and challenging them to think about and change their own behaviour and attitudes.

If the primary/secondary transfer arrangements had more consciously anticipated the kinds of problem which arose.

If he had received more focused and systematic assistance for his writing, as distinct from being given remedial reading.

If the curriculum had more sensitively supported him in his sense of identity, had helped him to make sense of who he was and what was happening to him.

If bodies such as Ofsted and QCA had ever given decent guidance to schools and teachers about identity and racism.

If.

Source: Derived from *This Is Where I Live: stories and pressures in Brixton*, Runnymede Trust, 1996.

Terminology

In summer 1998 local authorities were still expected to use the categories of the national 1991 census. For some communities in London, the census terminology made reasonably good sense. For most, however, it was unhelpful and misleading. The large Somali community in London, for example, was rendered invisible and uncounted, as also were longstanding Turkish communities. Further, the figures requested in February 1999 by the DfEE in relation to the Ethnic Minority Achievement Grant did not explicitly refer to pupils from refugee and asylum-seeking families, and the significant needs of such pupils were not recorded.

In 1991 there was a category named as 'Black'. This was subdivided into 'African', 'Caribbean and 'Other'. Subsequently, when statistical tables relating to the census were published, these three sub-categories became known respectively as 'Black African', 'Black Caribbean' and 'Black Other'. By the late 1990s the first of these, 'Black African' had become almost entirely useless for monitoring purposes in London, since it conflated a number of extremely disparate communities – for example, it made no distinction between Somalis and, say, Nigerians. The term 'Black Caribbean' makes ready sense to statisticians, but is virtually never used by the people to whom it actually refers. For this reason it is not used here, and ought not to be used in any other publication either. Instead, the term 'African-Caribbean' is used. The term 'Black Other' does not have a precise meaning even for statisticians let alone for any of the people to whom it supposedly refers. Different local authorities use it in different ways. For some, it means mixed heritage. For others, it includes also pupils defined by their parents or by themselves as 'Black British'. Some authorities barely use it at all, for they classify all mixed heritage and Black British pupils as African-Caribbean. In the following tables it is not used.

The terms used for South Asian communities in the 1991 census were Bangladeshi, Indian and Pakistani. This terminology was on the whole satisfactory. The term 'Indian' conflates Panjabi and Gujarati communities, however, with the consequence that it means different things in different parts of London. In Ealing and Hounslow, for example, 'Indian' primarily means Panjabi. In Brent and Harrow it primarily means Gujarati. The resulting ambiguity is unfortunate, but is not statistically serious in the pages which follow.

The category 'Chinese' was included in the 1991 census. It is broadly satisfactory. But since the actual number of Chinese pupils in London schools is quite low, extreme caution must be exercised in the interpretation of percentages about them. Chinese pupils are not included in the pages which follow.

The DfEE asked that all other pupils should be classified under the heading of 'Any other Minority Ethnic group'. Some authorities rightly insisted on counting and reporting on specific communities, for example Turkish, Turkish-Cypriot, Kurdish, Albanian and Vietnamese communities, and communities from the Middle East and South America. But plainly the category as a whole is of no practical use in relation to monitoring achievement, and it is not used in the following pages.

Definitions of achievement

For Key Stage 2, the DfEE asked for information on what proportion of pupils had reached Level 4 in mathematics and in English. It may be that the omission of science was a significant failure, as also the omission of the concept of average points score. A number of authorities do in fact monitor science results by ethnicity, and do collect average points scores. It would be valuable if, in future years, all other authorities – and the DfEE itself – followed their lead.

At GCSE, the DfEE asked for three pieces of information:

- The percentage gaining five A*-C passes: this is a widely used indicator of the minimum success required at 16+ to be able to start proceeding towards higher education. For monitoring achievement by ethnicity, however, it may be misleading, since for some groups it gives information about only a small number of pupils.

- The percentage gaining at least one A*-G: subtracted from 100 this shows the percentage gaining no qualifications at all. This is an extremely low level of achievement, and does not discriminate statistically between ethnic groups. It is not used in the following pages

- Average points score per pupil: this valuably complements the figures about percentages.

What the figures show – summary

Study of Key Stage 2 and GCSE results in summer 1998, in about 20 different London authorities, shows:

- At Key Stage 2, *in most but not all authorities*, the achievement of African-Caribbean pupils is well below the national average. The difference is even greater in mathematics than in English.

- At Key Stage 2 English, *in some authorities*, African-Caribbean achievement is at or higher than the national average

- At GCSE, in all authorities, there is a substantial difference between the achievement of African-Caribbean students and the national average. In some authorities proportionally more than twice as many White students achieve five A*-Cs as do African-Caribbeans.

- *Both* at Key Stage 2 (and both in English and mathematics) *and* at GCSE, Indian pupils have significantly higher achievement that all other groups in their LEA, and are generally achieving above the national average, particularly at GCSE. Also – though the raw figures are much smaller – Pakistani pupils in some parts of London are achieving at or above the national average.

- In most (but not all) of the LEAs studied for this report, the achievement of Bangladeshi pupils was lower than that of White pupils. In virtually all it was higher than that of African-Caribbean pupils.

Detailed figures relating to GCSE (five A*-C grades) are shown in Table 1 for thirteen London authorities – here given fictitious names in order to avoid invidious or misleading comparisons. These thirteen were chosen for inclusion because they all presented their GCSE data in the same way, and because all had submitted it at the time that this book went to press.

The national average in 1998 was 46 per cent achieving five GCSE passes at grades A*-C. Table 1 shows that in twelve of the thirteen authorities the achievement of Indian pupils was substantially above this. In the case of the thirteenth ('Laycock'), Indian achievement was precisely the same as the national average. The raw figures relating to Bangladeshi and Pakistani pupils (not shown in the table, for not all authorities reported them) were all fairly low, and the percentages must therefore be treated with caution. That said, the table shows that in most London authorities Pakistani pupils have higher achievement than White pupils and that, in five of the thirteen, Pakistani achievement is above the national average. The picture for Bangladeshi pupils in London is more varied, but generally Bangladeshi achievement is lower than White achievement.

The percentages for Caribbean achievement in Table 1 are all based on substantial raw figures so are definitely likely to be statistically significant. In every authority they are substantially lower than the authority's own average. Also, even more seriously, they are all substantially lower than the national average. The poorest results are in 'Kewdale', where only 12 per cent of African-Caribbean students achieved five GCSE grades A*-C in 1998, followed by 'Bridgeley', 'Heathington' and 'Galton', where the percentages were 18 or 19, i.e. considerably less than half the national average. In all four of these authorities African-Caribbean pupils are by far the largest single minority ethnic group. They are also, incidentally, the largest minority group in most of the other authorities featured in Table 1. The table as a whole shows dramatically the scale of African-Caribbean under-achievement in London – and therefore in Britain, for 60 per cent of all African-Caribbean people in Britain live in London. Further, it in effect shows why this book has been written, and why it is principally concerned with raising the achievement of African-Caribbean pupils.

Key Stage Two

For ten of the thirteen LEAs listed in Table 1, figures are available for English and Mathematics at Key Stage Two (i.e. the end of primary education.) These are shown respectively in Table 2 (English) and Table 3 (Mathematics). Several points of considerable interest arise, particularly when attainment at Key Stage Two (KS2) is compared and contrasted with attainment at GCSE.

Table 1

Percentages of students achieving five GCSE A*- C grades by ethnicity in 13 London LEAs, 1998

LEA	Bangladeshi	Caribbean	Indian	Pakistani	White	LEA
Amsden	26	23	-	-	42	35
Bridgeley	37	18	56	41	33	30
Coombe	35	23	57	41	33	38
Donwell	25	26	60	32	42	43
Edgemond	30	31	52	37	24	31
Foreworth	-	23	56	41	25	30
Galton	38	19	56	30	43	29
Heathington	36	18	-	67	26	23
Islip	-	26	62	61	38	50
Jaythorn	-	32	62	51	50	53
Kewdale	29	12	54	62	43	27
Laystock	25	23	46	39	41	35
Mansfield	71	30	55	58	39	46

Notes

All these LEAs are in London apart from one, which is an urban authority close to London. They have been given fictitious names to avoid invidious or misleading comparisons. All have substantial proportions (i.e. between 30 per cent and 60 per cent) of Black and other minority pupils. A blank indicates that the raw figure is too small for a percentage to have meaning. The national average in summer 1998 was 46 per cent.

Table 2

Percentages of pupils achieving level 4 at Key Stage 2 English by ethnicity in 10 LEAs, 1998

LEA	Bangladeshi	Caribbean	Indian	Pakistani	White	LEA
Amsden	62	70	71	-	75	69
Bridgeley	58	58	82	68	69	64
Donwell	57	71	73	52	64	65
Galton	45	48	66	68	51	57
Heathington	49	53	62	50	63	57
Islip	-	68	75	70	67	63
Jaythorn	-	58	77	66	76	74
Kewdale	57	54	64	53	63	55
Laystock	37	56	93	59	63	61
Mansfield	67	58	68	58	72	66

Table 3
Percentages of pupils achieving level 4 at Key Stage 2 Maths by ethnicity in 10 LEAs, 1998

LEA	Bangladeshi	Caribbean	Indian	Pakistani	White	LEA
Amsden	49	66	56	-	73	62
Bridgeley	58	37	79	52	63	56
Donwell	57	47	65	43	52	53
Galton	48	43	66	70	54	60
Heathington	37	39	56	50	59	51
Islip	-	53	69	64	60	57
Jaythorn	-	40	69	53	68	65
Kewdale	45	37	55	53	58	48
Laystock	31	48	87	44	59	54
Mansfield	42	39	60	42	62	57

As with GCSE results (Table 1), it is relevant to use national averages rather than local averages as the fundamental yardstick for comparison. In 1998 the national average for KS2 English was 64 per cent achieving Level 4 or above. The first thing to note about Table 2 is that six of the ten LEAs achieved this. This is in stark contrast to the situation at GCSE – Table 1 shows that only two out of the thirteen authorities under consideration were at or above the national average. Are pupils in London primary schools considerably better at English than their counterparts in other parts of the country? Are pupils in London secondary schools, however, considerably under-achieving? Is it perhaps the case that large numbers of children who attend an LEA primary school in London do not then transfer to an LEA secondary school in the city? At present the answers to such questions have to remain speculative. But this striking phenomenon, of a dramatic decline in London between attainment in primary education and attainment in secondary, needs to be borne in mind in the discussion which follows. It appears to affect African-Caribbean pupils much more than others.

In three of the ten LEAs included in Table 2, African-Caribbean attainment in English was higher than the national average. In another three, it was within six percentage points of the national average. This is in striking contrast with the situation at GCSE, where African-Caribbean attainment was nowhere near the national average in a single one of the LEAs under consideration. In so far as it is appropriate to consider attainment in KS2 English as an adequate indicator of all-round academic potential, it is clear that the gap between African-Caribbean attainment and the national average widens considerably in the course of secondary education.

However, attainment in KS2 English may not be an adequate indicator of potential. An implication to be drawn from Table 3 is that attainment in Mathematics is much more relevant. The national average for KS2 Mathematics in 1998 was 58 per cent reaching Level 4 or above. This was achieved by African-Caribbean pupils in only one ('Amsden') of the ten authorities listed in Table 3. In only one other ('Islip') was African-Caribbean attainment within five percentage points of the national average. This poor attainment by African-Caribbean pupils in Mathematics is all the more striking when one notes that in seven of the ten authorities under consideration the LEA average was close to or above the national average, and that in eight of them the attainment of White pupils was at or above the national average. **It would appear from Table 3 that attainment in primary mathematics by African-Caribbean pupils is a matter requiring urgent and focused attention**.

Table 4

Differences between African-Caribbean and national attainment in KS2 English and GCSE, 1998. All figures are percentage points.

Authority	Difference between African-Caribbean and national average, KS2	Difference between African-Caribbean and national average, GCSE	Increase in the differential
Amsden	+6*	-23	29
Donwell	+7*	-20	27
Islip	+4*	-20	24
Kewdale	-12	-34	22
Bridgeley	-6	-28	22
Galton	-3	-24	21
Heathington	-11	-28	17
Laystock	-8	-23	15
Mansfield	-6	-16	10
Jaythorn	-6	-14	8

*The plus sign indicates that African-Caribbean attainment in these authorities was above the national average at KS2.

With regard to South Asian communities in London, there is no evidence of a decline in relative attainment in the course of secondary education. In nine of the ten authorities under consideration (the exception was 'Heathington', where raw figures were in any case too low for percentages to have significance), KS2 attainment by Indian pupils was at or higher than (often much higher than) the national average in both English and Mathematics. Table 1 shows that this high attainment continued through secondary education. For Pakistani and Bangladeshi pupils at KS2 the picture is more varied. But it is clear from Table 1 that Bangladeshis in London narrow the gap between themselves and the national average in the course of their secondary education, and that Pakistanis wholly close it. These trends make the under-attainment of African-Caribbean pupils in secondary education all the more poignant.

Table 4 shows the differentials between African-Caribbean pupils and the national average at Key Stage 2 English and at GCSE in ten separate authorities, and shows also the increase in the differential in each instance. All the figures are percentage points. So in the first authority in Table 4 ('Amsden'), for example, African-Caribbean pupils were six percentage points ahead of the national average in English at Key Stage 2. At GCSE, however, they were 23 percentage points behind. So they had fallen back 29 percentage points altogether. Of course, Table 4 is mathematically rather crude, since it uses percentage points in relation to two different national yardsticks, 64 per cent for English at KS2 and 46 per cent for GCSE grades A*-C. The crudeness in fact masks the seriousness of the situation. An analysis which took accurate account of the mathematically different yardsticks would show an even greater comparative decline in African-Caribbean attainment in the course of secondary education.

'If you're White you're all right, if you're yellow you're mellow, if you're brown stick around, but if you're Black get back.'
American playground chant

Points arising

One of the most striking points arising from Tables 1-4 is the marked difference between local authorities. In 'Kewdale' only 12 per cent of African-Caribbeans achieved five GCSE passes at grades A*-C. But in three other authorities, 'Edgemond', 'Jaythorn' and 'Mansfield', the proportion was at least 30 per cent. There are three possible reasons for such differentials. First, they could be related to social class factors in different African-Caribbean communities in different parts of London – African-Caribbeans in 'Edgemond', 'Jaythorn' and 'Mansfield' may be much less affected by deprivation and disadvantage than those in 'Kewdale'. Second, they could be due to the fact that standards generally in these three authorities (as shown in the column for LEA average in Table 1) are higher than in other authorities. Third, the race equality policies in these three authorities could be more effective. It is impossible, on the basis of the information available, to judge which of these three explanations is the most probable.

The differences between authorities mean that blanket statements about African-Caribbean attainment, either nationally or London-wide, must always be treated with extreme caution. For example, as this book goes to press DfEE ministers have stated (press release dated 10 March, and article in *Daily Express* dated 8 March) that 29 per cent of African-Caribbean students nationally achieved five grades A*-C in summer 1998. Table 1 implies that this is likely to be substantially inaccurate and misleading so far as London schools are concerned. It is incidentally the case that of the twenty local authorities which have the largest numbers of African-Caribbean children and young people of school age, fifteen are in London.

Helplessness

In many LEAs there is an uncertainty which verges on helplessness about what are effective strategies to improve attainment for some groups. There is, for instance, a worrying ignorance, generally, about how to raise the attainment of Black Caribbean boys.

Ofsted, *Raising the Attainment of Minority Ethnic Pupils*, 1999

The DfEE does not require LEAs to analyse GCSE results by ethnicity in specific subjects, for example in English, mathematics and science, nor does it require LEAs to study D grades (for example) by ethnicity. Relatively few LEAs, in consequence, have collected and published such data. This double omission by both central and local government is most unfortunate. Individual schools, however, have taken a lead on these points. One of the important findings at one school, in this respect, is that African-Caribbean students have a preponderance of D grades, particularly in the three core subjects. If these findings were widely replicated, the task of massively improving African-Caribbean achievement, as measured by GCSE grades A*-C, would become entirely feasible and realistic.

A number of individual LEAs and schools routinely analyse GCSE results by length of enrolment at the secondary school where the exams are taken. The figures show very substantial differences between students who have spent all five years of secondary education at the same school and all other students. They are rarely or ever, however, cross-tabulated with ethnicity. If, as is quite probably the case, African-Caribbean students are more likely to change secondary schools than other students, this may well be a factor contributing to their under-achievement. This topic, like many others touched on in these pages, requires additional research.

Schools which take part in the national YELLIS scheme (Year Eleven Information System), run by a team based at the University of Durham, are able to analyse 'value added' by ethnicity. A school which recently engaged in such analysis found a strikingly large degree of progress amongst its bilingual students, particularly girls, but 'negative value added' (i.e. lower attainment in GCSE than was predicted by tests taken at the start of Year 10) amongst students, including African-Caribbean students, for whom English is the mother tongue. The precise reasons for such differentials require further research, including action research at school-level, to identify successful new approaches and measures.

Box 7

The features of inclusive schools*

Leadership

A strong and determined lead on equal opportunities is given by the headteacher.

Listening

Inclusive schools listen to, and learn from, their pupils and their pupils' parents, and try to see things from the pupils' point of view.

Parents and community

Inclusive schools create and maintain careful links with parents and local communities.

Persons as individuals

Inclusive schools try to understand and work with 'the whole child' – they are concerned with the personal, emotional and social development of each individual as well as with academic attainment.

Curriculum

Inclusive schools find and create opportunities, within the framework of the national curriculum, to show recognition and respect for their pupils' and students' cultural, ethnic, religious and linguistic identities.

Combating bullying

Inclusive schools have clear procedures for dealing with racist bullying and racist harassment.

Preventing exclusions

Inclusive schools put great stress on strategies to prevent exclusions, both fixed-term and permanent.

Expectations

Inclusive schools have high expectations of both teachers and pupils, and clear systems for targeting, tracking and monitoring the progress of individual pupils.

Monitoring

Inclusive schools monitor by ethnicity to see whether all groups are achieving equally; to identify unexpected shortcomings in provision; and to target specific areas for attention.

*These are the principal conclusions in *Making The Difference: teaching and learning strategies in successful multi-ethnic schools* by Maud Blair and Jill Bourne et al, published by the Department for Education and Employment in 1998.

Inclusive society

This book is essentially about the features of inclusive schools, as summarised in Box 7. But in the background, so to speak, there is the concept of an inclusive society – inclusive schools contribute, it is reasonable to expect and intend, to the development of an inclusive society. The features of such a society have been summarised in a submission made by the United Kingdom government to the United Nations, and in a recent speech by the Home Secretary. Extracts from these two documents are quoted in Box 8.

Box 8

Vision of a good society – the official UK view

'It is a fundamental objective of the United Kingdom Government to enable members of ethnic minorities to participate freely and fully in the economic, social and public life of the nation, with all the benefits and responsibilities which that entails, while still being able to maintain their own culture, traditions, language and values. Government action is directed towards addressing problems of discrimination and disadvantage which prevent members of ethnic minorities from fulfilling their potential as full members of British society.'

Source: UK submission to the United Nations Committee on the Elimination of Racial Discrimination (CERD), 1995.

'Wherever we come from, whatever our roots, or our faith, we all have a stake in being British and we can be proud of that. Celebrating diversity and building a fairer, more confident, multicultural nation with a fresh, strong sense of national identity is an important and timely project. Having confidence in yourself and holding on to a dream of what you can achieve is so important. Nothing should hold you back in reaching your full potential. I want a society that gives you these chances, a society where each of you, regardless of colour or race or religion has an equal opportunity to succeed. It is your future and we need to hear from you.'

Source: The Home Secretary speaking to Black teenagers, 17 March 1999

The true test of democracy, said the American author Ralph Ellison, is 'the inclusion – not assimilation – of the Black man.' The concept of inclusion provides a simple basis for comparative research and review, for it enables a series of empirical questions to be researched and answered. Comparisons can then be made between different places – between different cities and local authorities, for example – or between different times in the same place. Key questions about inclusion are whether Black and other minority people do in fact take part, in numbers commensurate with their numbers in the population as a whole, in the principal areas of public life:

- **party politics**, as candidates, elected members, activists and staff

- **public administration**, as civil servants, members of public bodies, local government officers, officers and members of health authorities

- **industry and commerce**, at all levels of management and responsibility

- **law and justice,** as judges, magistrates, barristers, solicitors, court officers, police officers, probation officers

- **education**, as teachers, governors, lecturers, administrators, inspectors, academics and textbook writers, and as successful pupils and students

- **the voluntary sector**, at all levels of responsibility, nationally, regionally, locally

- **the arts**, as creators, performers, critics and administrators

- **science and medicine**, as researchers, technologists and consultants

- **the media**, as reporters, editors, producers and columnists.

An inclusive society has four main features. In addition to (1) social inclusion itself, as distinct from social exclusion, the hallmarks are (2) equal opportunities as distinct from discrimination, both direct and indirect (3) peaceful resolution of conflicts as distinct from violence and discord (4) attitudes of mutual respect and recognition as distinct from prejudice and hostility. The four features interact with each other and influence each other. They can be shown in a simple visual diagram, as in Box 9.

Box 9

Components of an inclusive society

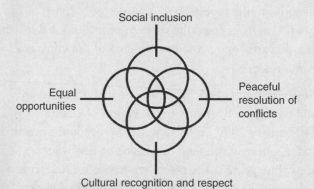

The term '**social inclusion**' refers to participation in society. It includes involvement in politics and in the economy, and in mainstream cultural life. Its opposite is '**social exclusion**' – the absence of Black and other minority people from key areas of social, political, recreational and economic life. Education in relation to social inclusion is concerned with equipping people with knowledge and skills, and also the paper qualifications ('educational achievement'), which they need for full participation in society. The wider political task is to combat poverty, inequality, unemployment, poor housing and poor health.

The term '**equal opportunities**' refers to fairness in the ways in which jobs, opportunities, goods and services are distributed in a society. Education in this respect is concerned with ensuring that all pupils and students have genuine access to the curriculum, and that none are at an unfair disadvantage, for example because their distinctive experiences, concerns and identities are disregarded. The wider political task is to create and enforce legislation against unfair discrimination, both direct and indirect, in all major areas of social life, particularly in employment.

The term **peaceful management of conflict** refers to respect for the rule of law, as distinct from engaging in violence and harassment. Education in this respect is concerned with developing skills of non-violent conflict resolution and, minimally, reducing or removing violence and harassment in schools. The wider political task is to ensure that the government itself respects human rights and that it minimises violence in relationships between communities.

The term '**cultural respect**' refers to attitudes ('the hearts and minds of people'), in particular attitudes of open-mindedness, interest and generosity, between different communities. Education in this respect is concerned with developing open-minded views of 'the self' ('us') and of 'the other' ('them'). The wider political task is to exercise cultural leadership, such that political leaders and the media influence public opinion in the direction of greater open-mindedness.

The opposite of inclusiveness: institutional racism

The Government's 1995 submission to the United Nations (Box 8) named the opposites of inclusiveness as disadvantage and discrimination. Four years later, in its response to the report on the murder of Stephen Lawrence, it accepted the concept of institutional racism as a powerful and accurate summary of the injustices to be addressed.

'Any long-established, White-dominated organisation,' said the Home Secretary to the House of Commons on 24 February 1999, 'is liable to have procedures, practices and a culture which tend to exclude or disadvantage non-white people. The police service in this respect is little different from other parts of the criminal justice system, or from government departments, including the Home Office and many other institutions'. Similarly, he could have added, the education system has procedures, practices and a culture which tend to exclude or disadvantage Black and other minority people, regardless of whether or not this is consciously intended. In the education system, to cite key terms in the Macpherson Report, there is 'a collective failure to provide an appropriate and professional service' to Black people. The failure is reflected in broad-brush statistics such as those shown here on pages 9-12, and also in millions of tiny episodes such as those described in the story of little Carl in Box 3, or evoked in the 'Life and life-chances' story in Box 5.

In a later section of this book, in Box 22 on page 32, there is an account of how the term 'institutional racism' was coined in the United States in the 1960s, and of how it has been used in Britain over the years. In Box 25 on page 37 there is a visual summary of the concept entitled 'The iceberg structure of institutional racism in education'. Throughout, the book is concerned with the tasks of removing procedures, practices and a culture in education which tend to exclude or disadvantage Black and other minority people, and with the tasks of replacing them with appropriate and professional services which are fair to all.

Concluding note: 'Only connect'

This book is about making connections – between inclusive schools and inclusive society, micro episodes and macro trends, school exclusions and social exclusion, identity and race, curriculum and relationships, the learning of teachers and the learning of pupils. In a current phrase, it is about 'joined-up policy-making', and 'joined-up' practical measures.

When E. M. Forster first used the phrase 'only connect', however, it was a rather different kind of joining-up he had in mind: 'only connect the prose and the passion', he said, 'and both will be exalted'. In the absence of such connectedness, he asserted, people are 'meaningless fragments' (*Howard's End*, chapter 22).

The struggle for racial justice, in Britain as elsewhere, needs to join up both prose and passion in Forster's senses – principles, rules, laws, policies, measures on the one hand, and energy, determination, anger, solidarity with pain and suffering, love, on the other. This book itself, accordingly, contains (a) much prose about management and planning and (b) snatches of poetry and poetic writing, and stories, anecdotes, conversations, brief quotations, tiny episodes, to evoke and express passion.

Exclude *v* 1 shut up or keep out (a person or thing) from a place, group, privilege, etc 2 expel and shut out 3 remove from consideration 4 prevent the occurrence of, make impossible

Exclusion *n* the act or an instance of excluding; the state of being excluded
From Latin *ex* (sense of going out, changing condition, completion) + *claudere*, shut, close, stop an opening
Synonyms: ban, bar, count out, eject, evict, expel, get rid of, ignore, keep out, leave out, omit, ostracise, remove, pass over, set aside, shut out, throw out.

2. IDENTITY

Inclusive schools respect the identities of their pupils
and students, and their experiences, histories and concerns.
They know where their pupils are coming from, and the tensions,
difficulties and struggles in which they are engaged.
This chapter notes that young people shape and choose
their identities amidst conflicting pressures and attractions.
It refers in particular to tensions relating to 'street cred',
culture and religion, racism, and the
concept of 'Britishness'.

Headings in this chapter

Boxes in this chapter

Uniqueness and belonging

The word 'identity' has two main sets of meanings. On the one hand, it is close to words such as distinctiveness, individuality, particularity, personality, self, singularity and uniqueness. On the other, it is close to words such as accord, commonality, correspondence, sameness, similarity, unanimity and unity.

At first sight, the two sets of meanings are contradictory – particularity *and* similarity, uniqueness *and* unity. In fact, however, the meanings are interdependent. For each person's identity is a unique mix of allegiances which they have in common with some, but not all, others. For example, someone might say: I am a Londoner, I am British. I am European, I am Jamaican, I am a member of the African diaspora, I am a woman, I am a mother, I live in Wembley, I was brought up a Methodist but am currently inclined to be agnostic, I am a teacher, I am a scientist, specifically I am a chemist, I support (not least since my daughters do) Queen's Park Rangers. The list could go on and on.

For everyone a list along such lines can be made of their allegiances, belongings and loyalties – the sources of their sense of identity. But no two lists are exactly the same. Also, various items on the list have different weightings at different times, and in different situations and places. There is therefore a sense in which a person's identity varies according to where they are and who they are with at any one time, and it changes over the years in the course of a person's lifetime. Your identity is formed partly by other people's perceptions and expectations of you, and by circumstances and inheritance over which you have no control. Partly it is formed by choices and decisions which you yourself freely make. Inevitably, therefore, identity involves conflicts, tensions and contradictions – for frequently you are pulled in different, perhaps even opposite, directions. To respect someone's identity is to take account of something multi-layered and ever-changing, and of the pressures they are under and the choices they may make.

An inclusive school, it follows, takes account of a wide range of allegiances and helps its pupils and students – and also its teachers and administrative staff – to hold them in balance. How a school does this in practice is seen in the curriculum (chapter 4 of this book), in its ethos and relationships (chapter 5), and in management and governance (chapters 6 and 7). Also, not least, it is seen in how it understands and addresses racism, both personal and institutional (chapter 3). In this chapter there is further discussion of identity in relation to four main themes:

*   youth identity and 'street cred'
*   cultural and religious identity
*   racism and identity
*   'national' identity

Youth identity and street cred

'Yu get mi miss, street life tough,' said a Year 9 boy recently to one of his teachers. 'An if yu nuh waan man tek step wid yu, yu afe bad it up. A don waan to be like dis, but a so it go.' His words were transcribed by the teacher, who also made an approximate translation: 'You understand, miss. Street life is hard. If you don't want people to take advantage then you have to be aggressive. I don't want to be like this, but I have to defend myself.' There is a fuller quotation from the boy in Box 10.

The boy vividly and poignantly reflects on his own life-story, and on the tension between the expectations of street culture on the one hand ('yu afe bad it up') and his own preferences on the other ('a don waan to be like dis'). Incidentally he gained a great deal of insight into himself and his situation through the process of telling his story, and benefited hugely from being able to talk reflectively to a sympathetic adult who listened rather than judged. All children and young people gain from being able to tell and reflect on their stories and life-experiences in such a way, and from being genuinely listened to by an adult whom they trust and like.

People inside us

The thing she was fussy about was all her ornaments. Ornaments from all around the world in that house. Huge Russian dolls, those ones that hide inside each other. Mrs Moody showed her one one day. It took up ten minutes to get to the baby hiding in there. The smaller they got the less detail on their faces. Mrs Moody said to her, 'We're all like that, aren't we? We've all got lots of little people inside us.' From *Trumpet* by Jackie Kay, 1998.

Box 10

Yu af fe play like yu a bad man

'Yu get mi miss, street life tough. An if yu nuh waan man tek step wid yu, yu afe bad it up. A don waan to be like dis, but a so it go. Yu get me, I wasn't always like dis, yu nuh, yo get me, I wasn't always like dis. Hear mi now aright. I use to live in P..., yeh, an ev'ryting was aw right. Nice neighbourhood, nice house an nice people. Nobody nah flex or bad up, they just nice. So you could I was nice den. Den wi af fi move to S... Wi only stayed a short time in S, an it was aw right. Den wi move to K. Dat was safe still, yo get me. Wi spend about two years in K, den wi move to R, an dats wen it stawt. Street life haad, yu get me, an man af fe survive, yu get mi. Yu af fe be a bad man. Yu caan be no pussy, yu af fe play like yu a bad man, or else man beat yu up an waan tek step a yu, yu get mi. Yo get mi, I don like being like dis, but a so go. If I was still in P I wouldn be like dis. Tings would be different yu nah. But in R yu af fe flex, yu af fe bu'n, be a bad man. Ev'ry one a fe tough it or man get yu.

Source: a Year 9 boy in a Pupil Referral Unit, London 1997, transcribed by one of his teachers. Reprinted here with permission.

Box 11

All this pressure

I was bad then. Really bad. I didn't want to do any school work. I just liked hanging out with my mates and having a spliff. I didn't stand a chance really. There was all this pressure on you not to do anything. Not to do well. Not to work hard. I mean practically every black guy my age that I saw on TV had just been arrested for something. Or was accused of mugging. It's like we only had the one face to them. The same face. The one that was wanted for something ... I've been picked up by the police countless times, man ... Just for being black and being in the wrong place at the wrong time.

Colman Moody, a character in *Trumpet* by Jackie Kay, 1998

The norms of youth cultures (both Black and White) are different in significant respects from the official norms and expectations of schools, to put it mildly. The principal points of tension are tabulated in Box 12. The purpose of the tabulation is to suggest that schools have a responsibility (a) to understand where certain of their children and young people are coming from – that is to say, to recognise and understand the features, pressures and attractions of youth cultures – and (b) to help young people make responsible choices between and amongst the pressures, expectations and requirements which they experience in their daily lives.

The features of youth cultures listed in Box 12 are by and large to be found in all communities in modern Britain (and also for that matter in many other European countries, and perhaps throughout the world), White as well as Black. But both White and Black youth cultures have additional distinctive aspects. In White youth cultures, for example, there is often vicious racism and a narrow sense of 'Britishness'. This point is referred to in greater detail later in this chapter. In Black youth cultures, there is much awareness of racism and disadvantage in wider society, and an expectation in consequence of being treated unfairly by authority figures, particularly the police. By the same token, schools and the education system are seen with profound distrust, and there is a sense that being successful at school involves 'acting White', at the expense of losing one's own core identity. For boys, success at school may be equated with losing one's masculinity.

'I was bad then. Really bad,' says a character in Jackie Kay's novel *Trumpet*, looking back on his teenage years. 'I didn't want to do any school work. I just liked hanging out with my mates ...' He links this rejection of school work directly to his experience of being Black in a White society, and to his negative encounters with the police. There is a fuller quotation in Box 11.

Box 12

Street Cred and School Norms – some of the tensions

With regard to:	Street Culture – expectations and norms	School Culture – expectations and norms
Demeanour, posture, gait, gesture, etc	Through body language show you expect to be respected – not messed with, not hassled or bothered, not provoked.	Through body language and your general attitude show you accept 'the role of the pupil' – you respect and defer to authority, tradition, the rules.
Provocation	Get your retaliation in first ... shoot from the hip ... swear and use verbal abuse .. signal you're ready to use force ... use force (fists, weapons) if necessary.	If provoked by a teacher, back down. Never swear at a teacher or threaten or use force. If by another student, try to keep cool, and don't fight.
Clothing and possessions	Use fashionable and expensive clothes and objects to show (a) that you are able to mobilise resources to secure them and (b) that you're confident no-one will dare to try to take them away from you. They show your personality, and that you are given respect.	Do not bring expensive clothing or possessions to school. They may induce envy in others, may provoke arguments and fights, may be a source of temptation. The school expects students to wear uniform, and/or generally to accept a dress code.
View of conflict	You win or you lose. Always try to win, or you'll lose face.	Official view is that winning and losing are for the sports field – and even there playing the game is more important than winning. In real life, seek resolutions of conflict in which no-one loses face.
Masculinity	You show you're a man by being hard, bad, cool – • Not being a swot or boffin (or whatever) at school • Not showing vulnerability, anxiety, tenderness, affection. • Showing contempt for homosexuality • Being respected, never losing face, defying authority • Taking risks, maybe dicing with death.	Manliness can include prowess in intellectual and artistic pursuits, physical prowess on the sports field, kindness and consideration in relationships, and taking on tasks of responsibility and leadership at school or in the community.
Views of outsiders	Anyone who doesn't conform is not allowed in.	Official view is that schools should be as inclusive as possible and should respect diversity and pluralism.
View of wider society	Society is unfair. The state's institutions are unfriendly and unhelpful. Some of them, particularly the police and indeed the whole criminal justice system, are hostile, unjust and repressive.	There's room for improvement, but basically society is seen as fair and decent. The police do a good job. Rules and laws are just and should be obeyed.
Role models and admired figures	Drawn from the worlds of popular culture, particularly music, style and fashion. Also sport, particularly football. Leaders of street gangs. Criminals.	Drawn from politics (national and world leaders), scientific invention and discovery, warfare, religion, literature and the arts.

Culture and faith

Tensions between street culture and school culture are not the only tensions which Black and other minority children and young people experience, and which schools need to attend to and respect. Also, there are tensions connected with religious, cultural and linguistic identity. Here too choices have to be made. Here too, to quote a character in a short story by Salman Rushdie (see Box 13), a proper response may be to 'refuse to choose', in other words to live with an unresolved tension rather than to deny it.

Choices of cultural identity, as also refusals to choose, are made within the wider context of much racism and xenophobia in wider society. This point was highlighted by the Runnymede Trust's 1997 report on Islamophobia. The report itemised seven main pressures on children and young people in Britain who have been born to Muslim families. A report on the choices open to Black children, or to children from other religious traditions (for example Hinduism or Sikhism), would similarly have needed to list many separate possibilities, influences and attractions. In Box 14 there is a brief summary of the Runnymede list. It is provided here (a) for its own intrinsic interest and importance and (b) because it is an example of the type of list which can be compiled for all minority children and young people in Britain today.

Box 13

Cultural identity – 'I refuse to choose'

...Was it that her heart, roped by two different loves, was being pulled both East and West, whinnying and rearing, like those movie horses being yanked this way by Clark Gable and that way by Montgomery Clift ...?

...I too have ropes around my neck, I have them to this day, pulling me this way and that, East and West, the nooses tightening, commanding, choose, choose. I buck, I snort, I whinny, I rear, I kick. Ropes, I do not choose between you. Lassoes, lariats, I choose neither of you, and both. Do you hear? I refuse to choose.

From *East, West* by Salman Rushdie, 1994

Racism and identity

White youth cultures may have all the features listed in the tabulation in Box 12. Also, they may contain vicious and explicit racism. Acceptance in such a culture may well depend on using, or any way not objecting to, racist conversation and behaviour. There is an important sense, therefore, in which racism may be part of a young White person's identity, for it is part of their identification with a group and a specific neighbourhood or territory. In the case of boys, it is part also, they believe, of their masculinity.

Induction into White racist sub-culture starts early. This point was cogently illustrated in an article which appeared in the *Daily Mirror* at the time of the publication of the Macpherson report in February 1999. The reporter, Brian Reade, visited an estate close to where Stephen Lawrence had been murdered. He watched a group of boys playing a game of kickabout football:

> The boys were no older than eight. White faces, cropped hair, decked out in top class Nike and Reebok gear, they whacked a ball against a garage door and chanted 'Shea-rer' every time they hit the metal goal. A typical Saturday morning sight, played out on council estates the length of Britain. But something caught my eye about that goal. No matter what angle the ball was struck, it hit a swastika. There were 17 of them, daubed on the garage next to the words PURE NAZI. Below was a huge Union Jack with the letters 'NF' scrawled at its heart.

The reporter went on to describe an eight-year-old boy reading some of the racist graffiti nearby, including a boast purportedly written by the person who had murdered Stephen Lawrence, and 'If they're brown knock em down. If they're black, stab em in the back'. He commented:

> Silence. The boy looked away bored, then strode back impassively to the game of football without flinching. There was no look of puzzlement at what he had just read. No confusion or discomfort. He understood it. He breathed it. He lived it.

It was part, the reporter could have added, of the boy's eight-year-old identity.

Box 14

Choices of cultural and religious identity – an example

The choice of Muslim as a self-definition may be not only a personal religious decision but also some or all of the following:

- a rejection of racist stereotypes in the majority population ('No more Paki. Me a Muslim,' says a character in novel by Hanif Kureishi set in the 1980s)

- an opposition to Western values ('pleasure and self-absorption isn't everything,' the character continues)

- part of a search for inner spiritual resources to withstand and combat racism and Islamophobia

- the shedding of an identity based on a specific country or region of parental origin

- the embracing of an identity which is seen on the contrary to be international and global, surpassing both Britain and (for example) South Asia.

The choice is made in awareness of some or all of the following influences:

1) **The family.** Muslim families, like all families, vary in their approaches to child-rearing and in the freedoms they permit to children and teenagers, and vary in their own loyalties and sense of belonging. Young Muslims, like all young people at all times and in all places, may be impatient or critical regarding some of their parents' loyalties and priorities.

2) **The mosque.** Up to the age of 14 most Muslim children attend a local mosque school. The pedagogical style is typically different from that which they encounter at their mainstream school, for it puts much emphasis on learning the Qur'an in Arabic by heart and on oral repetition (*tartil/tajwid*), and gives relatively low priority, in the first instance, to discussion and intellectual understanding.

3) **Muslim youth organisations.** There are many national, regional and local organisations which seek to promote understanding of the Muslim faith within the setting of a non-Muslim country such as Britain. For many young Muslims there may be a disparity between what they hear and learn from such organisations and what they learn at the mosque school or in their families.

4) **The Islamophobic messages of the mass media.** These often have the effect of undermining young people's self-confidence and self-esteem, their confidence in their parents and families, and their respect for Islam. Islamophobia can make extremist organisations, however, appear attractive.

5) **The largely secular culture of mainstream society.** This is encountered through the education system and the mass media, and in employment and training. Mainstream western culture is largely indifferent to all forms of religious commitment, not only to Islam.

6) **Street culture.** There are trends amongst some young British Muslims, particularly those who are unemployed or who expect to be unemployed, towards gang formation and anti-social conduct. Such trends exist everywhere in the world where young people feel dispossessed and disadvantaged.

7) **Extremist organisations.** Their discourse is frequently anti-western and their messages can be attractive to young people, since they appear to give a satisfactory picture of the total world situation. However, they have far fewer active supporters than the mainstream media claim.

Source: these notes are derived from *Islamophobia: a challenge to us all*, Runnymede Trust, 1997.

Box 15

Identity and teenage racism – six points from research

1) Adolescent racism is part of an adolescent sub-culture, both male and female, and is bound up with young White people's sense of identity and self-worth. It often exists independently of parents. ('If people of our age had the vote,' a teenager told the researchers, 'the BNP would get in easily round here because all the young people would vote for them.')

2) Youth workers and teachers working with White adolescents need further training on how to recognise and address the social base of racism in the teenage sub-culture as well as on how to focus on racism directly.

3) White adolescents often seek to justify their racism on the grounds that they themselves are treated unfairly by teachers, youth workers and police officers, whereas Minority Ethnic people, they claim, receive preferential treatment. A White girl is quoted as saying: '... I had a fight with a girl, right. She was Turkish and she said to me first, 'Yer White ice-cream head', and I said 'Shut up, you Turkish delight'. I got done for racism, she didn't ... They're allowed to say 'yer White this or White that' and we can't say anyfing back.'

4) Perceptions of unfairness such as this are in their essence false, but nevertheless the ways in which anti-racist policies have been promulgated and implemented have sometimes contributed to them.

5) There needs to be a thorough-going review of anti-racist policy, discourse, presentation and practice, and a re-focusing of energies and resources.

6) It is realistic as well as desirable for teachers and youth workers to develop 'white anti-racist youth cultures', as the term might be. There is much valuable potential, in this respect, in popular culture, particularly music, and in sport, particularly football.

Source: derived from *Routes of Racism* by Roger Hewitt, Trentham Books for Greenwich Council, 1997.

A local education authority which has done more than most to tackle such racism in White children and young people is the one where that boy lives, Greenwich. There is a summary in Box 15 of key findings in its publication *Routes of Racism* by Roger Hewitt, and from a follow-up project which took place under the auspices of the European Commission's *Cities Against Racism* project in 1995-98. A key point to stress is that White youth culture does not have to be racist. On the contrary, there are many example of anti-racist White youth cultures, and of Black, Asian and White teenagers taking a common stand against racism, shoulder to shoulder, both in the classrooms and playgrounds of their schools and on the streets of their neighbourhoods. Further, there are many examples of teenagers fashioning together new 'hybrid' sub-cultures, often revolving around music, which draw on a range of different traditions and streams.

Members of White racist youth cultures frequently cite Britishness as part of their identity – 'Keep Britain White' is one of their recurring slogans and rallying cries. The links between certain notions of Britishness and Whiteness were well expressed in the play *Ooh Ah Showab Khan* by Clifford Oliver. In Box 16 there is an extract from a speech made by one of the characters, Lenny, protesting against the involvement of Black and Asian players in British football. It summarises well a viewpoint which the curriculum of schools needs to confront and correct.

Box 16

'Stand up if you're proud to be British!'

Stand up if you're proud to be British! Stand up if you're proud of your British heritage. This land of ours, our fatherland, was fought for by our fathers and their fathers before them. Are you prepared to sit back and watch it destroyed by lefties, homos and foreigners? Are you prepared to watch while cheap foreign labour steals the work from our men and the bread from the mouths of our children? ... Football is our national game. The British game. We gave it to the rest of the world ... Keep Britain White – keep Blacks and Asians out of football!

A character in *Ooh Ah Showab Khan* by Clifford Oliver, 1998.

'National' identity

The character quoted in Box 16 ('Stand up if you're proud to be British!') expresses his understanding of British identity, and his belief that to be British is to be White. People who are not White, he apparently believes, simply *cannot* be British. A more common view is that 'Britishness' should be inculcated in all children and young people in British schools. 'TEACH THEM TO BE BRITISH' ran a headline in the mid-1990s, reporting with enthusiastic approval on a speech made by the chief executive of the School Curriculum and Assessment Authority (SCAA, latterly the Qualifications and Curriculum Authority, QCA). Headlines in other papers about the same speech included 'Teach All Pupils to be British', 'Putting Britain Back in the Classrooms', and 'It's Time to Teach our Young how to be British'. The speech, said the *Daily Mail*, set SCAA 'on a collision course with the race relations industry and left-wingers, by insisting the multicultural approach to education should be swept away and replaced by a national sense of identity and purpose'.

Such calls for a sense of national identity in education, and against so-called multiculturalism, are frequently made. Box 17, consisting of extracts from an editorial in the *Daily Telegraph* in December 1997, shows the flavour and gist of the arguments.

The views quoted in Box 17 are widely held. They do not help to build an inclusive curriculum or an inclusive society, however, even though their proponents claim that an inclusive society is what they want. On the contrary, the function in practice of such discourse is to exclude and disadvantage large numbers of Black and ethnic minority children and young people in British schools, and to miseducate many millions of White pupils. This point is made satirically by Michael Rosen in the extract which appears in Box 18.

Box 17

'Multicultural madness' – a point of view

The doctrine of multiculturalism in schools is becoming a threat to the stability and well-being of British society ... In many state schools, British culture and history and the Christian religion have been downgraded to the point where they are regarded as an embarrassment...

This is damaging to children's sense of the worth of themselves and of Britain. It is wrong for them to be denied a wholly justifiable pride in the achievements of this country. It is absurd for teachers, in their desire to be tolerant, to promote religions and cultures that in many respects are not tolerant at all. Some of these religions treat the subjugation of women and the murder of apostates as articles of faith. It would be idiotic for British culture to be so tolerant of other cultures that it faded into insignificance while promoting ways of thinking that, in some cases, are barbaric.

The greatest danger of all lies in immigrants being encouraged to see themselves as perennially aggrieved outsiders rather than as British. That is the road towards ghettos, division and violence. Schools should be part of the way in which our society develops common reference points, ways of thinking and a shared identity. Teachers need to spend less time promoting the worth of other cultures and more in understanding the value of our own.

Source: Editorial in *Daily Telegraph*, 15 December 1997.

Box 18

'This way, children' – a comment

This way, children, eyes to the front. I'm your new Britishness teacher, specially trained to give you your Britishness lessons. It's a bright new idea from the people who gave you those little SATs you did last month, and they got the idea from one of our greatest ever prime ministers ... and she told us back in 1978 that 'the British character has done so much for democracy, for law, and done so much throughout the world, that if there is any fear it might be swamped' – I'm talking, Rashida, please don't interrupt. Where was I? – 'people are going to react and be rather hostile to those coming in.'

Source: article by Michael Rosen in *The Guardian*, 1995

Tasks for schools

A way ahead, on this issue of 'national' identity in an inclusive society, was proposed in 1993 by the Runnymede Trust publication *Equality Assurance in Schools: quality, identity, society*. It is summarised in Box 19. Then in a later chapter, chapter 4, the approach is illustrated at length with regard to each separate subject in the National Curriculum. But first, in chapter 3, it is relevant and indeed essential to consider the key concept of racism.

TEACH THEM TO BE BRITISH

The Daily Mail, 18.7.95

Box 19

'Self' and 'Other' – teaching about identity

All human beings have to make choices amongst and within the heritages to which they have been born, and in which they take part. Such choices are made within certain parameters and constraints, of course. They are nevertheless real, and therefore have to be periodically renewed and confirmed, or periodically critiqued, changed or discarded. The issue is not only what to choose but how to choose, and having chosen how to live with the consequences. How to picture and value 'the Self'? How to represent and anticipate 'the Other'? These are the key questions.

*Equality Assurance in Schools** put forward the proposition that children and young people need assistance, guidance and support, in relation to the images of Self and Other which they make, of three main kinds. A person's identity needs to be:

confident, strong and self-affirming, as distinct from uncertain, ashamed or insecure;

open to change, choice and development, as distinct from being unreflective, doctrinaire and rigid;

receptive and generous towards other identities, and prepared to learn from them, as distinct from feeling threatened and hostile, and wishing to exclude or to be separate.

*Source: *Equality Assurance in Schools: quality, identity, society*, first published by Trentham Books for the Runnymede Trust in 1993, and frequently reprinted.

A useful life

To summarise, an essential task for schools is to help pupils choose their identity, and also 'to refuse to choose'. Amongst other things, this involves helping pupils to develop 'hyphenated identities', as the term sometimes is – Black British, British Muslim, London British, Indian British, and so on. At the same time, it involves remembering that culture is certainly not the only aspect of identity. This point is vividly stressed in the quotation in Box 20, referring as it does to gender issues and feminism, and to aspects of personality and personal energy, confidence and determination. The last sentence in Box 20 can readily be adapted. For example: 'He went forward, a Black man, to live a useful life in white England.' The notion of 'going forward, to live a useful life in white England' is a succinct and down-to-earth way of summarising many key educational objectives.

Box 20

A useful life in white England

... I thought what a terrific person she'd become ... there was in her a great depth of will, of delight in the world, and much energy for love. Her feminism, the sense of self and fight it engendered, the schemes and plans she had, the relationships – which she desired to take this form and not that form – the things she made herself know, and all the understandings this gave, seemed to illuminate her tonight as she went forward, an Indian woman, to live a useful life in white England.

Source: *The Buddha of Suburbia* by Hanif Kureishi, 1990

Go forward

We know at this point that we have to accept the inevitable that things are wrong. ... Before people can go ahead and make changes, we have to admit what is wrong. It is no use blaming each other for what has gone wrong in the past. We have to look forward... This is a very small place, this world of ours. We have to live together and we now have to say: let us put the past behind us, join hands and go forward.

Neville Lawrence, at the end of the day's hearings at the final meeting of 'The Stephen Lawrence Inquiry', Birmingham, 13 November 1998

Parallel universes

...She also complained of the parallel universes which black and white people in Britain inhabited. Both sides were visible to her as the child of a mixed marriage ... Her mother's family's advice to her as a child - that if she was lost she should seek out a policeman - was the opposite of that offered by her father's family, that 'if you are black, a white policeman can seriously damage your health.'

Report in **The Guardian** *(30.3.99) of speech by Oona King MP in the House of Commons, in a debate on the Macpherson Report*

3. RACE

In this chapter there is explanation and discussion of how the terms 'race' and 'racism' are used in this book. The chapter focuses in particular on the concept of institutional racism. It explains how the concept is used in the Stephen Lawrence Inquiry report and then applies it to the education system. The chapter also contains notes on the origins of racism and on the distinction which is sometimes made between 'colour racism' and 'cultural racism'. It ends with discussion of, and guidance on, dealing with racist incidents in schools.

Headings in this chapter

Boxes in this chapter

'How White Britain treats Black Britain'

The play *The Colour of Justice* was based on transcripts of the Macpherson Inquiry into police handling of the murder of Stephen Lawrence. It portrayed not only a catalogue of errors, failures and discourtesies on the part of individual police officers but also, in the words of one reviewer, 'how White Britain treats Black Britain'. There is a slightly longer quotation from the review in the grid of quotations which appears as Box 21. Also several of the other quotations in Box 21 are connected with *The Colour of Justice*. All are concerned with Stephen Lawrence's murder, and with the issues for British society – not just for the police service or for the criminal justice system – which the murder and its investigation raised. They form the backdrop to this chapter as a whole.

To say that race should be high on the educational agenda is to say that 'how White Britain treats Black Britain' is a fundamental question for everyone involved in education – headteachers and classroom teachers, education officers, elected members, inspectors, civil servants, school governors, teacher trainers. The report by Sir William Macpherson concluded that the unprofessional conduct of police officers was due not merely to inefficiency or to a chapter of accidents, but to what it called institutional racism. 'There must be an unequivocal acceptance,' said the report, 'of the problem of institutional racism and its nature, before it can be addressed, as it needs to be, in full partnership with members of minority ethnic communities.'

When he introduced the report in the House of Commons on 24 February 1999, the Home Secretary observed that institutional racism is a feature of all government departments, and all areas of society: 'Any long-established, White-dominated organisation is liable to have procedures, practices and a culture which tend to exclude or disadvantage non-white people. The police service in this respect is little different from other parts of the criminal justice system, or from government departments... and many other institutions.' The education system – amongst many other systems – stood accused. This chapter considers the concept of institutional racism, and applies it to education. First, though, it recalls the nature and origins of racism as a belief-system and as a political system.

Racism as a belief-system

As a system of beliefs, racism has three main components:

1. The belief that the human species consists of separate 'races', each with its own genetic and cultural features. There is no basis in science, however, for supposing that the human species consists of different races, each identifiable through signs such as skin-colour, hair texture, facial features, and so on. The belief that races exist, each race having its own cultural characteristics and physical appearance, was developed by scientists in the past. The belief is now totally discredited. Biologically, the human species shares a common gene pool. Studies of DNA have proved that there is much more genetic variation within each so-called racial group than between groups.

2. The belief that one race (for example, the so-called White race) is superior to other races.

3. The belief that it is therefore legitimate for the superior race to enslave or dominate members of other races, to discriminate against them, to exclude them from full membership of society, and to insult and abuse them.

This belief-system developed in its European and North American forms hand-in-hand with the development of colonialism and slavery, and at the present time is intricately connected, as both cause and consequence, with the economic situation of Black and other minority communities in modern Europe. There are further notes on the origins of racism below.

BLACK

Atrocious, depressing, dismal, distressing, doleful, foreboding, funereal, gloomy, hopeless, horrible, lugubrious, mournful, ominous, sad, sombre; dingy, dirty, filthy, grimy, grubby, soiled, sooty, stained; angry, furious, hostile, menacing, resentful, sullen, threatening; bad, evil, iniquitous, nefarious, villainous, wicked.

The New Collins Thesaurus, 1984

Box 21

Racism in Britain today – voices and perceptions

How White Britain treats Black Britain

Most of all *The Colour of Justice* demonstrates the role played in our society by unconscious racism. It isn't about a few bent coppers. It's about how white Britain treats Black Britain. As a Black woman said to me in the interval: 'It's not enough for a white person to say 'I am not a racist'. You have to ask yourself if other people find you racist.'

Review in Independent on Sunday, 17 January 1999

Every Black person

The death of Stephen Lawrence and the heroic struggle for justice waged by his family stands as a tragic epitaph to the racism that deeply poisons the British criminal justice system and the utter failure of the police to take such crimes seriously. The failure to deliver justice to Stephen's family is a denial of justice to every Black person in Britain.

Dave Weaver, Bandung Institute

Didn't know before

Edmund Lawson QC: *You referred to the victims of the assault, Stephen Lawrence and Duwayne Brooks, as the two coloured lads?*

Detective Inspector Bullock: *Yes.*

Edmund Lawson QC: *Do you understand that using the expression coloured is regarded as offensive?*

Detective Inspector Bullock: *I didn't know that before, sir.*

– Transcript of the Inquiry

All of us

To tackle institutional racism means saying that all of us in the organisation from the very top to the bottom are part of the problem.

Herman Ouseley, Commission for Racial Equality

More than this

It doesn't matter how much a Black person tries to explain his or her feelings in a racist society, those who are listening will continue to believe that there is no such thing as racism and that everyone is treated the same. Their reasoning is 'we have Black friends, and we have Black neighbours, so we are not racist'. It takes more than this to show whether you are racist or not.

Doreen Lawrence, on the last day of the inquiry

Civil rights movement

The inquiry has opened many people's eyes to the reality and extent of police racism. We now have to build on this awareness and develop a civil rights movement, which will work in a united, non-sectarian manner. If the momentum is to continue we need to develop monitoring groups as an integral part of the process. We cannot ask the Lawrences to lead the movement for another five years.

Southall Monitoring Project

Origins of racism

Racism exists in all societies throughout the world. Whenever human beings are in conflict they tend to 'racialise' each other – that is, to believe that they and their opponents belong to wholly different groups, with nothing in common. For it is easier to wage war against people and to try to conquer and dominate them, if you believe that they are totally different from yourself. The most convenient signs or markers of difference, when you are in conflict with someone, are those which are immediately visible, for example skin colour or facial features. If your enemy has the same physical appearance as yourself, however, you have to use other markers of difference – religion (as in Northern Ireland), culture (as in the former Yugoslavia), language, and so on.

In European countries and in the Americas and Australia, racism has been part and parcel of world history over the last five hundred years. From about 1500 onwards until the 1950s and 1960s, European countries dominated most of the countries of Africa and Asia. Profits from slavery, and from cash crops and new markets, helped to fund new manufacturing industries and economic development ('the industrial revolution') and modernisation. Noting that the inhabitants of the countries which they conquered and exploited tended to have darker skins than themselves, and needing to justify their superior power and riches, Europeans developed the twin notions that (a) skin colour is a marker of significant difference and that (b) people with lighter skins, themselves, had the right to dominate others. The idea that a darker skin colour is a marker of low status may have been derived from observations made within Europe entirely independently, in the first instance, of colonial expansion and conquest. For in each European country people with high status often had lighter skins than their compatriots, since they had sufficient wealth and power to spend more time indoors, sheltered from the sun and wind. It is also perhaps relevant to note that in most or all European languages, probably as a consequence of complexion being considered a sign of someone's social standing and power, there was a metaphorical correspondence between fairness and physical beauty, and between darkness and dirt, and darkness and danger. Europeans were thus already pre-disposed, before the age of expansion and conquest, to use skin colour as a marker or proxy of social standing and power. This tendency was then hugely reinforced by colonialism and slavery over the next 400 years.

Still influential

The age of colonial domination is now over. But the beliefs about 'race' to which it gave rise are still powerfully influential. This is partly because the beliefs are maintained by imbalances and injustices in the world trading system which have continued to exist even though the older forms of colonialism have largely disappeared. But it is mainly because people from the former colonies were encouraged to come to Europe in the 1950s and 1960s, in order to do various kinds of menial work which the indigenous populations were no longer willing to do themselves for the wages on offer, for example in the textiles and steel-making industries, and in transport and health services. The colonial belief that these people were inferior to White Europeans helped to justify discrimination and even violence against the newly arrived immigrants. Racist beliefs, narratives and attitudes have continued in circulation to justify the marginalisation and social exclusion of Black people and many other minority and migrant people throughout European Union countries.

The targets of racism in Europe at the present time include not only communities from outside Europe which have been settled here for 50 years or more but also substantial numbers of refugees and asylum-seekers who have taken up residence much more recently. Refugees have suffered considerable trauma and disruption, have severe difficulties in finding employment and housing, and have few rights to welfare benefits or political representation. In addition to these disadvantages, there is profound hostility towards them in the mass media, which often uses metaphors of 'flooding', 'pouring in', 'rising tide', 'waves' and so forth. Further, refugees are frequently attacked, physically or verbally, on the streets and in their homes. Such hostility frequently appears to be a coded and indirect attack on long-established communities as well.

Racism's two strands

In other European Union countries it is customary to use the phrase 'racism, xenophobia and antisemitism' as a way of summarising the evils to be tackled. The phrase is an awkward mouthful and is unlikely to become widespread in Britain. It is, however, helpful. For it stresses that hostility based on skin-colour and physical appearance is not the whole picture. Also there is hostility based on differences of culture, language and religion – i.e. xenophobia and antisemitism. Over the centuries this latter strand has targeted Gypsies, Jewish people and Muslims within Europe, and also a range of cultural, linguistic and regional minorities. Both forms of prejudice are usually present. But frequently one or the other is dominant.

The terms 'colour racism' and 'cultural racism' are sometimes used to refer to these two main forms of prejudice and hostility. Another way of referring to the same distinction is to speak of 'north-south racism' (Europe-Africa, also the northern-southern distinction in the United States) and 'west-east racism' (Europe-Orient, or Christendom-Islam). This formulation has the advantage of being easily memorable and accessible. It also helps to draw attention to the currently most serious form of cultural hostility in Britain, Islamophobia. But of course so simple an idea can all too readily lead to unhelpful simplifications. The essential point to stress is that over the centuries racism has had two separate but interlinked strands.

Until recently, the one strand (colour racism) affected mainly relationships between Europeans and people outside Europe, in the various colonies, whereas the other (cultural racism) mainly affected relationships within Europe, between the dominant majority culture and various minorities. Nowadays, since the migrations to Europe of the 1950s and 1960s, the two strands are frequently intertwined.

Markers of supposed difference: an example

The distinction between physical and cultural markers of difference is strikingly introduced by the main character, Shahid, in *The Black Album* by Hanif Kureishi. Shahid is a British Pakistani who grew up in a mainly White area of England. In this self-description he begins by referring to physical markers of difference, particularly his skin colour:

> 'Everywhere I went I was the only dark-skinned person. How did this make people see me? I began to be scared of going into certain places. I didn't know what they were thinking. I was convinced they were full of sneering and disgust and hatred. And if they were pleasant, I imagined they were hypocrites. I became paranoid. I couldn't go out. I knew I was confused and ... fucked up. But I didn't know what to do.'

This is a poignant description, from the anguished victim's point of view, of crude colour-racism. But as Shahid continues, it is clear that there is more to his predicament and anguish than exclusion and discrimination based on skin colour alone. The issues are to do with cultural inclusion, belonging and superiority as well as physical appearance:

> 'There's a much worse thing ... I don't think I can talk about it. But perhaps I should ... I wanted to be a racist ... My mind was invaded by killing-nigger fantasies ... Of going around abusing Pakis, niggers, Chinks, Irish, any foreign scum. I slagged them under my breath whenever I saw them. I wanted to kick them up the arse... I wouldn't touch brown flesh, except with a branding iron. I hated all foreign bastards ... I argued, why can't I be racist like everyone else? Why do I have to miss out on that privilege? Why is it only me who has to be good? Why can't I swagger around pissing on others for being inferior? ... I have wanted to join the British National Party ... I would have filled in the forms – if they have forms ... How does one apply to such an organisation?'

Box 22

Institutional racism – the term's history

The term 'institutional racism' was coined in the United States in the 1960s and came into widespread use following the publication of *Black Power: the politics of liberation in America* by Stokely Carmichael and Charles Hamilton. Officially, racism was no longer part of American law – it was no longer institutionalised. But racist attitudes, assumptions and beliefs were still, it was argued, embedded in American institutions and in White American culture. Therefore it could be said that not only individuals but also institutions can act in racist ways – i.e. if they treat Black people less favourably than White people, and if they therefore perpetuate and exacerbate inequalities between White people and Black in relation to goods such as health, education, property and power.

Further, the argument was that institutions can act with racist effects even when individuals in those institutions neither realise this nor intend it. Racism could only be eliminated, it followed, if there were significant institutional changes. The term 'institutional racism' was a deliberately provocative way of saying that major changes were still required throughout American society. Carmichael's arguments were particularly directed against White liberals, for he perceived that White people who had supported the Civil Rights Movement were now relaxing their efforts against racism. He defined how he was using the term semantically. Also, he made it clear that in coining and using this new term he was giving voice to the feelings and perceptions of very many Black people in the United States, and that he had a political, not just a semantic, analytic or philosophical agenda.

The term quickly crossed the Atlantic and was applied to British situations. There was no recent history of segregation as official government policy but nevertheless the concept made sense to campaigners. Here too it gave voice, in a convenient shorthand way, to people's feelings and perceptions. Here too it was a shorthand way of evoking a political programme. In the field of employment law it was translated into the legal term 'indirect discrimination' and incorporated into the Race Relations Act. However, the term 'indirect discrimination' was by no means a complete translation of what Carmichael and other campaigners had in mind.

Lord Scarman

In 1981 Lord Scarman referred to institutional racism in his report on the Brixton disorders. He is widely believed to have said that there is no institutional racism in Britain. His exact words are worth quoting, however, for in certain respects he has been misrepresented. His essential point was a semantic one, and involved distinguishing between two possible meanings of the term under consideration:

> 'It was alleged by some of those who made representations to me that Britain is an institutionally racist society. If by that is meant that it is a society which knowingly, as a matter of policy, discriminates against Black people, I reject the allegation. If, however, the suggestion being made is that practices may be adopted by public bodies as well as by private individuals which are unwittingly discriminatory against Black people, then this is an allegation which deserves serious consideration and, where proved, swift remedy.'

Lord Scarman's second meaning was close to what Stokely Carmichael had intended – except that Carmichael, of course, was in no doubt that indeed public bodies are frequently discriminatory in their actions. Scarman wrote also as follows:

> 'Institutional racism [in the first of the two separate senses mentioned above] does not exist in Britain; but racial disadvantage, and its nasty associate racial discrimination, have not yet been eliminated. They poison minds and attitudes: they are, and so long as they remain will continue to be, a potent factor of unrest.

Stephen Lawrence Inquiry

Subsequently a number of academics argued that the concept of institutional racism, in Lord Scarman's second sense, is not clear enough to direct policy or to underpin research. The term was nevertheless retained by campaigners, as a shorthand term to articulate their feelings and outlook. It came again into prominence in 1998, as is now well known, when it was used by a range of witnesses at the Stephen Lawrence Inquiry, in allegations against the Metropolitan Police.

Please note: some of the definitions and explanations considered at the Stephen Lawrence Inquiry are quoted in Box 23.

Racists want to kick 'any foreign scum', not just (so to speak) people with darker skins than themselves. For the markers of inclusion and exclusion, and of superiority and inferiority, are cultural as well as physical. Kureishi notes and shows that the racist's motivation is to belong and to feel superior – to belong to a cultural entity, deriving self-respect from being included in 'us', not excluded in 'them', and deriving profound satisfaction from feeling sure that one's own cultural traditions are superior to those of others. Shahid even feels it would be better to be in the BNP ('I would have filled in the forms – if they have forms ... How does one apply to such an organisation?') than to be an excluded outcast.

Connections and components

Earlier in this book (page 15) it was suggested that at an inclusive society has four main components. Similarly racism may be thought of as having four main components: (a) exclusion (b) discrimination (c) violence and (d) prejudice. These four components overlap with each other, and feed into each other. They can be visualised in a simple diagram, as shown in the box below. Action against racism and xenophobia – in education as in social policy more generally – involves action against all four components.

The four main components of racism

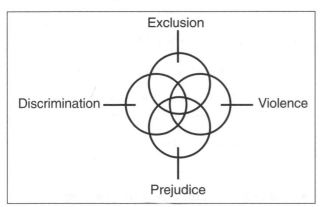

The term 'exclusion' refers in this context to the absence of Black people from key areas of social, political, recreational and economic life. The term 'discrimination' refers to procedures and customs which treat Black and people less fairly than White people. The term 'violence' refers to attacks – and includes verbal abuse, threats and insults as well as assaults. The term 'prejudice' refers to false beliefs about White superiority.

Institutional racism

Box 22 recalls the history of the term 'institutional racism' – the phrase that was coined in the United States in the 1960s, quickly crossed the Atlantic, was considered by Lord Scarman in 1981, was not taken on board at that time by policy-makers, came again into prominence during the Stephen Lawrence Inquiry, and was this time accepted by the UK government as a valuable and powerful concept. Sir William Macpherson and his advisers considered a range of possible definitions and explanations of the term. Several of these are quoted in Box 23.

Anti-racist education

Key terms and phrases in Box 23 can be used to compile a statement about racism in education, as follows:

> In the education system there are laws, customs and practices which systematically reflect and reproduce racial inequalities ... If racist consequences accrue to institutional laws, customs and practices, a school or a local education authority or a national education system is racist whether or not individual teachers, inspectors, officers, civil servants and elected politicians have racist intentions ... Educational institutions may systematically treat or tend to treat pupils and students differently in respect of race, ethnicity or religion. The differential treatment lies within an institution's ethos and organisation rather than in the attitudes, beliefs and intentions of individual members of staff. The production of differential treatment is 'institutionalised' in the way the institution operates.

Institutional racism – approaches to a definition

Box 23

'Organisational structures, policies, processes and practices which result in ethnic minorities being treated unfairly and less equally, often without intention or knowledge'. (*Commission for Racial Equality*)

'Laws, customs and practices which systematically reflect and reproduce racial inequalities in society. If racist consequences accrue to institutional laws, customs and practices, the institution is racist whether or not the individuals maintaining those practices have racist intentions.' (*Commission for Racial Equality*)

'The way institutions may systematically treat or tend to treat people differently in respect of race. The addition of the word 'institutional' therefore identifies the source of the differential treatment; this lies in some sense within the organisation rather than simply with the individuals who represent it. The production of differential treatment is 'institutionalised' in the way the organisation operates.' (*Professor Simon Holdaway*)

'A generalised tendency, particularly where any element of discretion is involved, whereby minorities may receive different and less favourable treatment than the majority. Such differential treatment need be neither conscious nor intentional, and it may be practised routinely by officers whose professionalism is exemplary in all other respects. Its most important challenging feature is its predominantly hidden character and its in-built pervasiveness within the occupational culture.' (*Dr Robin Oakley*)

'**The collective failure of an organisation to provide an appropriate and professional service to people because of their colour, culture, or ethnic origin. It can be seen or detected in processes, attitudes and behaviour which amount to discrimination through unwitting prejudice, ignorance, thoughtlessness and racist stereotyping which disadvantage minority ethnic people.**' (*Stephen Lawrence Inquiry*)

Source: all quotations are from Chapter 6 of The Stephen Lawrence Inquiry (Macpherson Report). The last is the definition adopted by the report itself.

In order to combat institutional racism in education, as thus defined, the concept of anti-racist education was developed in Britain by community activists and practising teachers, often supported by local authorities and teachers' unions, in the 1970s and 1980s. It had five main aspects:

- Robust refusal even to reflect, let alone to reproduce, 'racial' inequalities

- Vigorous commitment to listening and attending to Black experience, Black stories, Black perceptions

- Review and change of laws, customs and practices in education, including those which are sanctioned or promoted by central and local government, which operate to the disadvantage of Black and other minority pupils, parents and communities

- Review and change of occupational culture, not least in the attitudes implicit in staffroom cultures towards African-Caribbean boys and towards non-'Western' traditions and heritages, particularly Islam

- Combating and reducing direct racism – violence, harassment, name-calling – amongst pupils in the playground.

POURING FOR 60 YEARS

'German Jews pouring into this country'

'The way stateless Jews from Germany are pouring into this country is becoming an outrage ...'

Daily Mail, 20 August 1938

'Why do we let in this army of spongers?'

'So many asylum seekers are pouring into this country ... that the authorities here are finding that they simply cannot cope...Word has travelled far about the generosity of our social security system, which they intend to milk while embarking, in many cases, on criminal activity.'

Daily Mail, 26 September 1998

Box 24

RACIAL INEQUALITY IN INSTITUTIONS – DIMENSIONS AND EXAMPLES

Dimensions of inequality	Examples of inequality in the criminal justice system	Examples of inequality in the education system
OUTCOMES White people receive more benefits than Black, and racial inequality is therefore perpetuated.	Crimes against White people are investigated and cleared up more effectively than crimes against Black people.	White pupils leave school at 16 or 18 with substantially better paper qualifications than Black pupils.
Black people receive negative results more than do White people and in this way too inequality is perpetuated.	Black people are far more likely than White to be stopped and searched by the police.	Black pupils experience punishments, particularly permanent and fixed-term exclusions more than White pupils.
STRUCTURE In senior decision-making and policy-making positions there are proportionately more White people than Black, and in consequence Black interests and perspectives are inadequately represented.	There are few Black officers at or above the rank of Inspector, and also few Black people in the rest of the criminal justice system.	There are few Black headteachers or deputy heads, and few Black education officers, inspectors, teacher trainers and textbook writers.
CULTURE AND ATTITUDES In the occupational culture there are assumptions, expectations and generalisations which are more negative about Black people than about White.	Black people are more likely than White people to be seen as criminals or potential criminals.	Black pupils are more likely than White pupils to be seen as trouble-makers, and to be criticised and controlled.
RULES AND PROCEDURES Customary rules, regulations and practices work more to the advantage of White people than Black.	Throughout the criminal justice system Black people are treated less favourably than White people.	The national curriculum reflects White interests, concerns and outlooks and neglects or marginalises Black experience.
STAFF TRAINING Staff have not received training on race and racism issues, and on ways they can avoid indirect discrimination.	Police officers have not been trained to identify and investigate racist attacks.	Neither initial not inservice training pays sufficient attention to race and racism issues.
FACE-TO-FACE INTERACTION Staff are less effective in communication with and listening to Black people than they are in interaction with White people.	Encounters between White police officers and Black members of the public frequently escalate into needless confrontation.	Encounters between White staff and Black pupils frequently escalate into needless confrontation.

Anti-anti-racism

There were – and are! – many thousands of anti-racist teachers, headteachers, governors and education officers. Anti-racist education had the potential to be widely influential following the publication of two major reports by central government in the early and mid 1980s, known respectively as the Rampton Report and the Swann Report. It came under sustained attack from leading politicians and from sections of the media, however, and was increasingly marginalised and de-emphasised following the Education Reform Act of 1988. An example of 'anti-anti-racism', as it is sometimes known, was shown earlier in Box 17, under the heading of 'Multicultural Madness'.

Those who led the attack on anti-racist education, and those who readily complied with it, did not express themselves with the kind of racist language cited above in the quotation from Kureishi's novel. The consequence of their attacks, however, was that significant efforts to reduce racial inequalities in education were not made. It was not until the introduction of the Ethnic Minority Achievement Grant in 1999 that central government even began to collect ethnically-based statistics on attainment, and not until the publication of the Stephen Lawrence Inquiry, also in 1999, that central government officially began to recognise that there is institutional racism in the education system, as in other public services.

Box 24 shows how, in general terms, the concept of institutional racism may be applied to education. The left hand column summarises general points in the Stephen Lawrence Inquiry report about the nature of institutional racism, and refers to six main dimensions: (1) outcomes, sub-divided into 'goods' and 'bads' (2) structures (3) culture and attitudes (4) rules and procedures (5) training and (6) face-to-face interaction. The middle column contains examples of institutional racism in the criminal justice system and is similarly based on the Stephen Lawrence Inquiry report. The right hand column gives examples in the education system.

This book, it is hoped, will contribute to the renewal – but also to the refocusing – of anti-racist education. In any such renewal and refocusing, it will be important to bear in mind the insights of the Stephen Lawrence Inquiry report, and also the points from anti-racist youth work in Greenwich which were summarised in Box 15.

Iceberg

A simpler approach to describing institutional racism in education is shown in the iceberg image in Box 25. It suggests that the high numbers of exclusions of African-Caribbean pupils are 'the tip of the iceberg'. The body of the iceberg is the substantial under-achievement shown in, for example, the statistical tables included in this book (see pages 9-12).

Teaching about race

In teaching about race, it is relevant to note that progress is possible, and that indeed progress has been made. In South Africa, to cite the most inspiring example of recent years, apartheid has been brought to an end. In the United States, the Civil Rights Movement in the 1960s led to substantial changes for the better. In Britain and several other European countries there are now laws against racial discrimination in employment, and high penalties for racist violence and harassment. There is still much to be done in Britain and in all other European countries, and there is absolutely no reason for complacency. It is important, however, that children and young people should appreciate that progress is possible, and that they themselves can contribute to it.

History syllabuses and programmes of study should include teaching about justice, equality and human rights and within this framework there should be reference to the Civil Rights Movement in the United States, and to similar struggles throughout the world, including campaigns and experiences over the years in Britain. Also, children and young people can help create, review and maintain anti-racist policies for their own schools, particularly with regard to behaviour in the playground. Further, they can consider issues of racism and behaviour in circle times and school councils, and in programmes of personal, social and health education; and they can get involved in projects such as Kick Racism Out of Football, and in the many areas of popular culture where there is a mingling of cultural traditions and styles.

There is fuller discussion of teaching about race in Chapter 4.

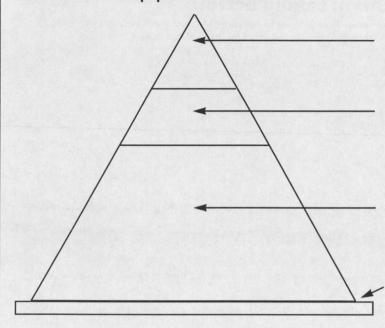

Figure 1: The iceberg structure of institutional racism in education – the case of African-Caribbean pupils and students

Box 25

The 'tip of the iceberg' – African-Caribbean boys are 3-4 times more likely to be permanently excluded from school.

The middle of the iceberg – African-Caribbean boys are far more likely to experience fixed-term exclusions, unofficial exclusions and internal exclusions.*

The bulk of the iceberg – African-Caribbean pupils are considerably more likely to leave school at 16 with poor or worthless paper qualifications.

The 'sea bed' – social exclusion and institutional racism in wider society.

*'Unofficial exclusions': when a parent is strongly advised to withdraw their child from a school. 'Internal exclusions': when a pupil is removed from their usual classroom, and required to work elsewhere on the school premises.

Dealing with racist behaviour

Most of this chapter has been about institutional racism not about direct racism. It is important, however, that every institution – and particularly every school – should have formal policies and procedures for dealing with direct racism when it occurs. The main features of such policies and procedures are outlined in Box 27. The poem in Box 26 is a poignant reminder of how extremely urgent and serious the issues are.

Concluding note

In its response to the Stephen Lawrence Inquiry report, the government has indicated that it sees teaching about race as part of citizenship education. This chapter has shown what the main subject-matter of courses about race and racism should contain. There is much fuller discussion in the next chapter. It refers to the whole curriculum, not to citizenship education only.

Box 26

They call you names

They call you names for the fun of it
To make your insides weak
To injure all your happiness
And tell you you're a Sikh

To them you are totally different
To them you are lower class
They'll hit you and hurt you as much as they like
Till your insides are eaten at last

They say you're brown and they hate you
And they never, ever go away
They've become a part of your life now
And I fear they are here to stay

Kiran Chahal, a pupil at Cranford Primary School in Hillingdon

Box 27

Racism in and around the school: taking action

1. In every school there should be a code of practice which outlines specific procedures to be followed for recording and dealing with racial harassment, as also with other kinds of abuse and bullying, on the school premises, and on journeys to and from school.

2. The record should include:

    •   a description of what happened

    •   names and ethnic backgrounds of pupils involved

    •   action taken to support the pupil(s) who was the target of the abuse or harassment

    •   action taken in relation to the perpetrator(s)

    •   whether parents were informed and if so in what ways

    •   whether a report was sent to the LEA

3. All pupils should be aware that there are school rules prohibiting racial harassment, abuse, graffiti and name-calling: in the playground, corridors and toilets, etc, and on journeys to and from school.

4. All staff, including administrative and support staff, need to be familiar with formal procedures for recording and dealing with bullying and racist incidents.

5. It is important that all staff are vigilant with regard to behaviour amongst pupils, and that they ensure that they are as familiar as possible with pupils' experiences of bullying.

6. Pupils themselves should be involved in drawing up and agreeing principles and codes of practice relating to bullying and harassment, and should play a part in dealing with incidents.

7. It is important that parents should be involved in agreeing principles and procedures for dealing with bullying and harassment, and in dealing with specific incidents.

8. There needs to be coverage within the curriculum of interpersonal behaviour amongst pupils, including racist name-calling and bullying, and this should be linked with wider issues of learning for citizenship and participation in society.

9. Staff should accept responsibility for helping to ensure that play and leisure areas encourage and promote positive and cooperative behaviour amongst pupils.

10. Guidance such as the following should be discussed and agreed:

    •   Act immediately when a racist incident takes place.

    •   Clear support should be provided to the pupil who has been insulted or rejected

    •   Make it clear to the pupil who was insulting that their behaviour was unacceptable.

    •   Help pupils settle elements in their argument or conflict which are unrelated to ethnicity, culture or religion.

    •   Explain that racist insults hurt. So, of course, do all insults. But racist insults are particularly and distinctively serious, for three separate reasons:

        i.   They are an attack on an individual's family, community and heritage, not just (so to speak) on aspects of their personality. They are even more hurtful, therefore, than other insults.

        ii. They therefore may have the effect of intimidating or threatening large numbers of people, not the specific individual under attack only.

        iii. They are serious because those who use them sometimes believe they are representing widely held views. It is essential, in this latter respect, that they should know their views are not in fact acceptable.

    •   So never side-step the issue with a response such as 'words don't hurt', or 'there's no difference between racial insults and other kinds of insult'. The old saying 'Sticks and stones may break my bones but names will never hurt me' is, quite simply, untrue.

    •   People at the receiving end of racist insults defend themselves in a variety of ways, including angry retaliation. Extreme care should be exercised when dealing with incidents involving retaliation, since otherwise the victim may be punished for retaliating while the perpetrator of the original insult may feel free to repeat the offence.

    •   Discuss racist incidents with parents so that they reinforce the school's anti-racist practices in the home.

    •   Be sure you give pupils correct information about so-called 'racial' differences and about issues to do with race equality, so that any myths, misinformation, distortions and bias can be countered. For example, races do not exist from a scientific point of view – the human species is a single race. Nevertheless racism, involving the belief that human beings do belong to different races and that some races are superior to others, continues to blight the lives of millions of people throughout the world.

4. CURRICULUM

If 'identity' and 'race' are to be higher up the educational agenda, as argued in chapters 2 and 3, what are the implications for the curriculum of schools? This is the central question addressed in this chapter. The chapter has two parts. First, it is concerned with content and subject-matter, and refers in this connection to every national curriculum subject, plus also religious education and personal and social education. Second, there is consideration of practical classroom methods, with particular regard to collaborative groupwork, language development and problem-solving.

Headings in this chapter

Boxes in this chapter

Themes and objectives

In every curriculum subject there are opportunities to engage pupils by showing respect for their cultural and personal identities. And in all there can be opportunities to teach and learn about the nature of racism, and about the principal actions and measures required to build greater racial justice. Some of the many possibilities are listed in the next main section of this chapter, 'Every curriculum subject'. Underlying them, there are five over-arching ideas:

1   The world in general, and also Britain in particular, contains much cultural, ethnic and religious diversity.

2   Underlying the diversity, all human beings have in common certain basic values, aspirations and needs.

3   Excellence is to be found in all cultures and traditions, not only in 'the west'.

4   There has been much borrowing, mingling and mutual influence over the centuries between different countries and cultural traditions.

5   The building of justice, including racial justice, within and between countries and communities, is of fundamental importance,

In Box 28 these five underlying themes are set out in the form of educational objectives, grouped into the conventional categories of knowledge, skills and attitudes.

USEFUL RESOURCES

Campaigns and concepts

Homebeats: struggles for racial justice is a CD Rom produced for Key Stage 3 and Key Stage 4 by the Institute of Race Relations (IRR) in 1997. It contains material on Africa, the Caribbean, South Asia and the United States as well as Britain, all attractively presented for research, enquiry and discussion, and accompanied by music, film, illustrations and quizzes. Users can readily make their own connections. Full details from IRR, address on page 86.

Role models

Tamarind Books is a publishing house specialising in producing fine classroom materials about Britain as a multi-ethnic society. Its **Black Profiles** series, published in summer 1999, contains six titles: Benjamin Zephaniah, poet and performer; Malorie Blackman, award-winning author; Lord Taylor of Warwick, barrister; Samantha Gross, orthopaedic surgeon; Jim Braithwaite, entrepreneur; Patricia Scotland QC, lawyer. Address for further information, page 86.

Box 28

Summary of objectives

Knowledge and Understanding

•   Knowledge of the history and development of one's own cultural traditions (including sub-cultural traditions, for example the norms of teenage youth culture), and of the ways in which these both foster and constrain one's own personal identity

•   Knowledge of 'race' – the origins of racism, aspects of European expansion and colonialism, migrations to Europe, race relations in Britain, action against racism

•   Knowledge of the physical, social and psychological needs which human beings have in common, including nutrition and shelter, and values relating to freedom, self-respect, belonging, and a sense of meaning and purpose

•   Knowledge of the various ways in which different cultures, communities and societies respond to these fundamental needs and moral concerns.

Skills

•   Ability to contribute to the development of mainstream public, cultural and political life, and to the affairs of one's own community

•   Ability to learn from different cultural experiences, norms and perspectives, and to empathise with people with different traditions

•   Ability to analyse and criticise features of cultural traditions, and to identify instances of prejudice, intolerance and discrimination

•   Ability to engage in discussion, argument and negotiation.

Attitudes

•   Willingness to sustain the positive aspects of one's own culture, and so to be constructively critical when appropriate

•   Willingness to learn from different traditions, cultures and identities

•   Willingness to challenge instances of prejudice, intolerance and discrimination

•   Willingness to accept reasonable and equitable procedures for resolving conflicts.

Our course takes us from Africa to the Caribbean and then to Britain; it travels from Zimbabwe to Jamaica to Brixton.
– course outline (KS3 history) at a London school

CURRICULUM ●

Every curriculum subject

In order to unpack the general points in Box 28 in further detail, here are about 60 statements which might appear in an Ofsted report. They are clustered according to the subjects of the national curriculum, with references also to religious education and personal and social education. The list as a whole can be used for reviewing the curriculum of any and every school.

Art

1   There is reference to excellence in a range of different cultural traditions, not only in 'the west'.

2   There is stress on cross-cultural borrowings and influences.

3   There is stress on common elements, concerns and strivings in different traditions, reflecting shared human values.

4   Visiting artists – painters, photographers, potters, sculptors, printmakers – are from a range of cultures and traditions.

5   Art is used to explore social and political issues.

6   Through art pupils express their own sense of personal and cultural identity.

English and Drama

7   Fiction, drama and poetry are drawn from a range of genres, times and places.

8   There is stress on values and concerns which all human beings have in common.

9   There is recognition of bias in literature and the media, and questioning of stereotypes, including racial, ethnic and cultural stereotypes.

10   There is stress on the differences between formal and informal English, and the importance of formal English for academic success.

11   Pupils use literature to explore social and political issues, for example racism and anti-racism.

12   Pupils use literature to explore issues of personal and cultural identity.

Geography

13   Pupils study differences and commonalities in humankind's relationship with the physical environment.

14   There is stress on global connections and interdependence.

15   Negative images of Third World countries are criticised or avoided.

16   Migration, population movement and settlement are seen as recurring features of human experience.

History

17   Pupils study differing perceptions of, and narratives about, the same event.

18   British history is taught within a world perspective, related to events in other countries.

19   There is teaching of key political concepts, including resistance, pressure, democracy, rights, equality, justice, citizenship.

20   There is study of local heritage, neighbourhood and community in such a way as to support all pupils' sense of personal identity and personal history.

21   Opportunities are taken to teach about struggles for racial justice, for example the Civil Rights Movement in the United States.

22   Pupils learn about the history of Black people in Britain, and the development of Britain as a multicultural society.

Cruel and forgetting

Not many

'At this time [about 1750] not many people thought there was anything wrong with slavery.' – *School textbook still in widespread use in the 1990s.*

Angry

'I am angry with this, because the author is forgetting the slaves were people too. They didn't want to be slaves for the rest of their lives. He did not even stop to think what he's writing about. I think he's cruel. He may not think there was anything wrong with slavery because it was not him who had to be a slave. If he was split away from his family he would not like that. That is exactly what happened to the slaves. He should be ashamed of himself writing this.' – *From an essay by a Year 9 student at a London school, 1990s*

Mathematics

23 Mathematics is seen as a universal human language, used in all cultures and societies.

24 Tasks, problems, materials and activities reflect the multi-ethnic and multicultural nature of modern societies.

25 Mathematics is used to analyse social, economic and political affairs.

26 Links are made with other subjects, to develop pupils' knowledge of themselves and the wider world.

Modern Foreign Languages

27 There is reference to cultural, social and historical contexts.

28 Contrasts and comparisons are drawn between different languages.

29 There is reference to borrowings and influences.

30 Bilingualism and multilingualism are seen as widespread throughout the world.

31 There are open and enquiring attitudes towards diversity within and between languages.

Music

32 Examples of excellence and high achievement are taken from a range of different cultural traditions.

33 There is reference to intercultural borrowings and influences.

34 There is stress on common elements, concerns and strivings in different traditions.

35 Visiting musicians are drawn from a range of backgrounds and traditions.

36 Pupils use music to explore aspects of personal identity, and social problems and issues.

Physical Education

37 Games and sport are seen as universal human activities.

38 There is stress on cooperation and sensitivity, fair play and respect, acceptance of rules and decisions, handling of success and failure.

39 Dance is used as a medium for exploring aspects of personal identity, and social and political issues.

40 Name-calling and racial abuse are seen as unacceptable in team games, including fixtures with other schools, as well as in all other aspects of school life.

Personal, social and health education

41 There is support for a range of personal and cultural identities amongst pupils and parents.

42 There is teaching about concepts of discrimination, prejudice, exclusion, harassment, injustice.

43 There is attention to pupils' own perceptions, experiences and concerns.

44 There are opportunities for reflection on events in the school itself, including bullying and racist name-calling.

45 There is stress on techniques and methods of conflict resolution which pupils themselves can use.

Religious education and collective worship

46 There is stress on common elements, concerns and values in different religious traditions.

47 There is stress on cultural, national and ethnic diversity within each religion.

48 There is critical reference to media misrepresentations and stereotypes, and of negative stereotypes in wider society.

49 There is stress on stories and teachings about tolerance and reconciliation.

50 It is acknowledged that religion is sometimes used to justify injustice or conflict.

Science

51 Processes of observing, hypothesising, reasoning and testing are seen as universal throughout all cultures, not as distinctively 'western'.

52 Resources, materials and activities which reflect the multi-ethnic and multi-cultural nature of modern societies are used.

53 There is reference to the use of scientific method in analysing social, economic and political affairs.

54 It is stressed that there is no scientific basis for supposing the human species is divided into separate races.

Technology

55 There is reference to the needs met by technology which all human beings, at all times and in all cultures, have in common.

56 Resources, materials and activities reflect the multi-ethnic and multicultural nature of modern societies.

57 There is stress on the importance and value of traditional technologies, and of alternative technology, but avoidance of negative images of 'less developed' countries.

58 The Internet is used to display and explore aspects of 'the global village', for example to make links with schools in other countries.

Please note: many of the ideas in this list are taken from *Equality Assurance in Schools: quality, identity, society,* published by Trentham Books for the Runnymede Trust.

For a wealth of curriculum materials reflecting international dimensions, see the catalogue issued by the Development Education Centre, Selly Oak Colleges, Bristol Road, Birmingham B29 6LE. Telephone 0121 472 3255.

Box 29

Planning an anti-racist course

A teacher describes a course in Year 9 History:
Our course started with one great strength. It was rooted in an explicit anti-racism with which the students identified. The course therefore actually had 30 great strengths, the 30 anti-racist students, black and white, of 9T. (If you count the teacher, 31.) They wanted to make the course work. They wanted to struggle with complex texts and demanding ideas in order to challenge or be challenged by them.

Wanting to was not, of course, enough. But it did help. The high level of motivation that the ideas within the course engendered, and the way in which these were unpacked, enabled me to spend more time reading sources to and with small groups or individuals, and putting materials on tape for people to listen to. It also led to a collectivity and sharing within the class that enhanced everyone's learning.

But the students were not going to go on 'wanting' unless they could succeed and see themselves succeed. Education for equality has to mean ways of learning and teaching that enhance the self-confidence of students, that encourage them to question, that foster a sense of collectivity, a sense that one's peers are resources, and that one is oneself a valuable and valued resource for one's peers. Didactic information-giving would be unacceptable ...

Having established my priorities for content, I had to marry the materials to a methodology that would allow everyone to have a sense of success. I was also determined to do this without patronising the students. I wanted to offer a richness of resourcing, richly scripted, richly structured, rich in text and context, in pictures and in imaging.

Yet I had to prevent the resources, or my marking, or our classroom, from saying 'But you are too poor, in vocabulary and in will, to engage with all this.' I had to find ways of helping the class take on difficult work and I needed to return to them images of their successes in doing so.

Source: description by a London teacher of a Year 9 history class, 'Black People in the Americas', 1990s.

Practical methodology

In Box 29 there is an extract from a paper about a Year 9 history course, 'Black People in the Americas'. The teacher who wrote the paper makes several vital points about practical methods and classroom organisation:

- The pupils learnt from each other as well as from the teacher, and from the resources which she prepared and provided.

- The pupils felt that they were given respect by the teacher, and by each other, and this was a major source of their motivation.

- The course engaged the pupils' sense of personal, cultural and ethnic identity, and also their sense of local space and neighbourhood within the wider world.

- The course involved much intellectual and cognitive challenge.

- The resources for the course included several which communicated non-verbally and imaginatively as well as directly.

- The pupils developed confidence in their own ability to grapple with, and make personal sense of, complex ideas, language and concepts.

A source of theory and practice

In the planning of courses which contain the features listed above, much can be learnt from good practice in the field of English as an Additional Language (EAL). This is not because the pupils one is teaching are bilingual – they may or may not be – but because EAL theory sheds light on the needs of all pupils. By the same token, practical EAL methodology is of use and value to all.

EAL specialists make two fundamental distinctions. On the one hand, they distinguish between everyday English (sometimes known in the academic literature as BICS – Basic Interpersonal Communicative Skills) and curriculum English (CALP – Cognitive Academic Linguistic Proficiency). The principal differences between everyday English and curriculum English are listed in Box 31.

Then also, a fundamental distinction is drawn by EAL theory and practice between high and low levels of cognitive challenge. The two sets of distinctions can be used to create a simple matrix, as shown below, referring to four different types of language use. The features of cognitive challenge are listed in Box 30.

Four types of language use

Register of English	Level of cognitive challenge	
	Low	*High*
Everyday	Type 1: for example, chat about everyday events and plans, and about TV programmes, pop stars, sports, etc.	Type 3: for example, talk within the context of structured exercises and activities which require genuine communication.
Curriculum	Type 2: for example, giving rote-learned answers, copying from books, doing 'comprehension' exercises.	Type 4: for example, writing answers in SATs and GCSE and written work in preparation for all such

Challenge and groupwork

All four types of language in the matrix (page 44) are important and valuable, for pupils and students of all ages. But it is particularly important that pupils should have plenty of opportunities to use what the matrix calls Type 3 language – interactive and collaborative, engaging their sense of personal identity, but with high cognitive demands. The route, so to speak, from Type 1 language (everyday conversation and chat) to Type 4 language (the kind required for high academic achievement and success in the national curriculum) has to involve spending a lot of time with Type 3.

In educational contexts, the two main features of Type 3 language are high intellectual challenge on the one hand and collaborative groupwork on the other. These features are described in greater detail in Boxes 30, 32 and 33. The first of these (Box 30) is a brief summary of problem-solving and thinking skills. It is rather abstract as it stands, but helpfully supports the planning and evaluation of practical, down-to-earth activities such as those mentioned in Box 32, on collaborative groupwork, and Box 33, on practical projects and investigations. The latter are suitable mainly for Key Stage 2, but can be adapted for both older and younger pupils.

Collaborative groupwork

There are many valuable suggestions and practical ideas in the publications of the Development Education Centre, Selly Oak Colleges, Bristol Road, Birmingham B29 6LE. Also useful are *Let's Cooperate* and *Let's Play Together*, both by Mildred Masheder, available from Green Print, 2 Rendlesham Mews, Rendlesham, Woodbridge, Suffolk IP12 2SZ.

Box 30

Problem-solving and thinking skills

1. Comparing, contrasting and matching

The vast majority of human knowledge depends, in the first instance, on observing and investigating similarities and differences. 'This goes with this', 'that goes with that'. The distinctive language includes concrete nouns, everyday adjectives, adverbs of comparison, and possessives. Key words and phrases include *like, similar, same, different, features in common.*

2 Categorising, classifying and sequencing

Out of activities of comparing, contrasting and matching there develops the process of categorising and classifying – phenomena are clustered, on the basis of their similarities and differences, into discrete groupings. If the phenomena are events, their classification will almost certainly involve sequencing. The distinctive language includes generic nouns, references to amounts and scale, and connectives and prepositions of time. Key words and phrases include *characteristics, criteria, belonging, arrange, sort.*

3 Speculating, hypothesising, inferring and predicting

Having placed phenomena into categories, human beings make conjectures and generalisations about the underlying patterns and reasons. The distinctive language includes terms and tenses expressing conditions. Key words and phrases include *why?, can we explain? what might be the cause? what would happen if? what would be the result if?*

4 Evaluating and selecting

Choices have to be made between alternative and perhaps competing explanations. The distinctive language may include adjectives for describing emotions. Key words and phrases include *good idea, agree, disagree, prefer, appropriate, fair, important, urgent, priority.*

5 Explaining and justifying

The chosen explanations are justified with evidence, and with reference to generalisations, principles and rules. Potential objections are refuted. The distinctive language includes terms of cause and effect. Key words and phrases include *because, it follows, therefore, nevertheless, although, however.*

Box 31

The features of curriculum English

	Everyday English – for example, a conversation between two children the playground	Curriculum English – for example, a child writing in history, science or geography
Motivation for using language	To communicate, or to maintain a relationship with a peer	To demonstrate knowledge and understanding
Relationships with others	Very important	Less important
Sense of personal identity	Very important	Less important
Expression of personal feeling	Very common	Rare
Subject matter – (a)	Usually of immediate interest and relevance	Seldom of immediate relevance
Subject matter – (b)	Often about things which can be seen as the talk takes place	Seldom about things which can be seen as the writing takes place
Subject matter – (c)	Often about a shared experience	Seldom about a shared experience
Possibility of feedback	Immediate feedback given by others on how well one is communicating	Feedback not immediate, and may take hours or even days
Importance of non-verbal communication – tone of voice, facial expression, posture, gesture, body language, etc	Extremely important	Of no importance
Nouns	Mostly one or two syllables, derived from Germanic or Anglo-Saxon sources	Many of two or more syllables, and derived from Greek, Latin or French
Pronouns	Clear from situation what they refer to	Clarity depends on observing grammatical rules
Technical terms	Seldom used	Must be used
Register	Frequent use of slang and colloquialisms	Formal language essential
Importance of Standard English	Often not important, particularly if others present use non-standard vocabulary and forms.	Essential

Source: *Enriching Literacy* by Brent Langauge Service, 1999

There is one thing I am certain about. Nobody is superior to anybody
– *Paulo Freire*

CURRICULUM ●

Box 32

Collaborative Groupwork – useful activities

1 One. two, four

Start by requiring each pupil to do or decide or write or choose something on their own. (If they write, provide a simple framework – a sentence-completion or writing-frame task, for example. And have them write in a box or on a slip of paper, not a large blank and maybe daunting sheet.) Then have them talk in pairs about what they have written or done. Then form fours or sixes.

2 From listening to writing

This is a simple *one, two, four* activity which has great value in helping to develop proficiency in curriculum language.

First, the teacher reads at normal speed a short key text. It could be an entry in an encyclopaedia, a book review, a passage in a textbook, a newspaper article or editorial, an extract from a guidebook, and so on. The pupils listen without making notes. Second, the teacher reads the text again and this time pupils make notes of key words and phrases.

Third, pupils work in pairs, comparing their notes and adding to them.

Fourth, the pupils work in fours. Again they compare notes and add to them. The essential task now, however, is to re-constitute the original text as accurately as possible.

3 Objects to handle

Arrange for pupils to work with things which are tangible and which they can handle and arrange. Moving their hands seems to loosen their tongues and their minds. For example, provide phrases, statements and quotations on separate slips of paper, or (preferably) on cards. Also, it is valuable to use three-dimensional objects. Specific tasks can include:

- sort the objects into pairs or into four (or whatever) categories, and use a dictionary or thesaurus to find a range of words which describe each category and differentiate it from others

- place the objects on a matrix or Venn diagram

- sequence the objects

- rank the objects according to specific criteria.

4 Precise tasks

Always give precise unambiguous instructions about the actual outcome you want. 'Here are pictures of six people. Choose the two people you would most like to meet. For each of them write down the two questions you would most like to ask them.' Tight and clear instructions, leading to an obvious outcome, are liberating rather than cramping. Vague instructions ('discuss what you think of this') can merely dissipate energy and interest, and lead to much waste of time.

5 Brainstorming

This well-known activity is frequently invaluable. It involves the making of a list without any discussion in the first instance. If it goes well, everyone feels able and willing to contribute, existing knowledge is activated and pooled, and an atmosphere of openness and mutual trust is established. Further, the list which is generated can be a valuable basis for various ranking and sequencing activities.

6 Collaborative drafting

In the 'real' world of adults a great deal of real discussion (talk as distinct from chat) happens around the drafting and re-drafting of papers. Such discussion can readily be replicated in classrooms. In addition to drafting real texts from scratch, there are plenty of other possibilities – including using writing frames, cloze procedure, sequencing text which has been cut up, adding sentences or phrases in the best place, choosing between alternative phrasings to express the same idea, and so on. Drafting and finalising a report on a collaborative investigation (for example the types of investigation listed in Box 33) is particularly valuable in schools, and particularly reminiscent of report-writing in the 'real' world.

Source: Enriching Literacy by Brent Language Service, 1999.

Exercises and activities – the example of diary writing

The *Homebeats* CD Rom (for details see useful resources on page 40) contains material on – among many places – Birmingham, Bradford, Brixton, East London, Glasgow, Liverpool, Notting Hill and Southall. The accompanying booklet contains a wealth of suggestions for practical exercises and activities. The titles of these include: Building communities, Stereotypes, Positive images and role models, Women's contributions, Systems of domination, Meanings of home, Identity – who we are, Vision for a better world and Write your own history.

The 'Building communities' activities include the following:

'Imagine you arrive in Britain in the 1950s from overseas (choose Africa, the Caribbean or South Asia). What would you find strange? Write a diary covering your last week in your country of emigration and your first week in Britain. Include your search for employment and housing.'

'Write a diary covering 10 yearly intervals. Your first entry could cover your arrival in Britain in, for example, 1955. Write another page dated 1965, another dated 1975 etc. up to the present day. What things have changed? Is the racism better or worse or different?'

The writing of such diaries was a feature of work in many British schools during 1998 in connection with the *Windrush* celebrations. The following extracts are from work at a primary school in south London. Then opposite, in Box 33, there are notes on many further projects which similarly involve collaborative groupwork and high levels of cognitive challenge, and which provide opportunities for achieving the objectives listed in Box 28.

Dear Diary

Today I arrived in Britain. I thought I would be arriving to a welcoming country but instead I saw signs saying, 'No Irish! No Blacks. Keep Britain White!' As I walked to my flat, a youth called me 'nigger!' I heard of a man called Oswald Mosley. He is a Fascist. Today he won an election. I'm so frightened that the Teddy Boys are going to beat me up.

Dear Diary

Today a Black man was found dead. His name was Kelso Cochrane. The Teddy Boys did it. I'm worried I'll get hurt. I wish I had never come to Britain. I wish Oswald Mosley had never been elected. Sometimes I want to call the names back but then I think No, I'm not going to stoop down to this level.

Dear Diary

Today the Blacks are building a Pentecostal church because the Whites won't let us in the English church. I am really happy because I can keep up my religion. And it will prove to the Whites that we are willing to fight for what we believe in.

Dear Diary

Today, on my way to work, I saw a sign saying: If you want a nigger neighbour, vote Labour. My heart sank. It was going to get worse. People are going to get hurt and, now the Conservatives are taking over, there are going to be more racist remarks.

Dear Diary

Today Enoch Powell gave a speech on T.V. He said, "In ten to fifteen years time, the Black man will have the whip hand over the White man." I can't believe he said that. Anyway, he got sacked.

Dear Diary

Today Enoch Powell supporters marched up and down the hill, chanting, "Enoch Powell!" over and over again. 88% of Britain supported him. The people who didn't support him were students. The police were stopping the students but not the Enoch Powell supporters. Is it all going to start again?

Box 33

Projects and investigations at Key Stage 2

- Make a sequence of images to illustrate an incident described in a local newspaper which raises issues to do with fairness, cooperation and cultural identity.

- Involve visitors who have a wide range of experiences and memories to talk about their childhoods and lives. Include reference to houses, shops and buildings close to the school and to where the children live.

- Make a collaborative portrait of members of the class, showing cultural and ethnic identities, and the variety of skin tones, hairstyles, clothing and eye colours.

- Enact stories at school assembly which involve repeated patterns of speech and behaviour, and which express symbolically the children's own feelings about identity, growing up, tensions and quarrels, friendships and cooperation.

- Use communication games and exercises which require children to listen and speak carefully to each other in pairs and small groups, and which involve handling visual and pictorial material reflecting cultural and ethnic diversity.

- Study pictures and artefacts from a particular village or town in another part of the world, and construct time-lines, maps, stories and graphs to show how people there live. Imagine what daily life is like for children in the chosen place. Write real or imaginary letters to the children who live there.

- In studies of how humans keep healthy, use images, examples and case-studies from a wide range of historical, geographical and cultural settings.

- Provide pictorial displays which show scientific activity (hypothesising, designing fair tests, predicting, theorising about causal links, etc) at all times in human history, and in a wide range of countries and cultures.

- In connection with studies of, for example, Athens and Sparta, draw up a charter or constitution for a democratic classroom in Britain in the 1990s.

- Devise a questionnaire asking other children about their likes and dislikes regarding the playground, and identify valuable changes which might be made.

- Organise a maths trail – a survey of a local street or area with questions requiring measurement, counting of specific features, presentation of results through diagrams and charts – so that children develop knowledge of their local neighbourhood as well as a sense of mathematical evidence.

- Conduct an opinion survey, for example about a selected range of television programmes which reflect cultural and ethnic diversity, and present tabulations of the results in a variety of numerical, graphic and pictorial styles.

- Use drama to enact and study ways in which language is used in everyday conversations and interactions to reflect status, seniority, respect and deference, and what it means to use language assertively as distinct from aggressively or submissively.

Reviewing language policy

Helping pupils move from everyday English to curriculum English (Box 31) is a task for every class or subject teacher. Additional staff appointed under the auspices of the Ethnic Minority Achievement Grant can most certainly make valuable contributions but cannot be solely responsible. A whole-school policy on promoting language development is therefore required. Box 34 lists features of good practice in this regard. It is presented in the form of a review questionnaire, so that it can be readily used in staff discussion.

Box 34

Reviewing language policy

	HOW ARE WE DOING?		
	1	2	3
	Poor	Making progress	Satisfactory
1 Proformas for lesson planning prompt staff to consider a wide range of practical activities and approaches.	☐	☐	☐
2 Activities are cognitively demanding, whatever the pupils' competence in English.	☐	☐	☐
3 Much use is made of visual material, particularly material which communicates key concepts.	☐	☐	☐
4 There is much use of practical and manipulative activities.	☐	☐	☐
5 There is focused attention to the development of writing skills.	☐	☐	☐
6 There is much use of collaborative groupwork.	☐	☐	☐
7 Pupils are grouped such that pupils at the early stages of learning English have opportunities to interact with native speakers.	☐	☐	☐
8 Much use is made as appropriate of pupils' home and community languages.	☐	☐	☐
9 There are clear procedures for welcoming new arrivals.	☐	☐	☐
10 All staff consciously aim to extend and enrich pupils' vocabulary.	☐	☐	☐
11 There is good attention to language awareness and knowledge about language.	☐	☐	☐
12 The concept of genuine partnership teaching is well understood by all staff and is widely implemented in practice.	☐	☐	☐
13 Parents are kept fully informed about the school's language policy relating to bilingualism and to English as an additional language.	☐	☐	☐

5. RELATIONSHIPS

An inclusive school has an inclusive curriculum, as outlined
in chapter 4. Also it is characterised by mutual listening and
respect – among staff, between staff and pupils,
among pupils. This chapter considers relationships
of various kinds, particularly between staff and pupils.
In its second half it considers the specific issue of
permanent exclusions from schools – i.e. situations
where a school considers that relationships
have irreparably broken down.

Headings in this chapter

Boxes in this chapter

Discussion and reflection

A book such as this cannot possibly lay down rules about relationships. It can, however, provide material for reflection and discussion. In Box 36, for example, there are nine short stories about things which happen in schools or things people say. Such stories invite discussion of short term, medium term and long term responses to the situations or events which they describe, and discussion also of the immediate and underlying causes. Then in a later box, Box 37, there is a list of situations specifically concerned with relationships in classrooms. These too invite discussion of a wide range of issues.

The chapter starts with quotations from a school where relationships seem particularly good – see Box 35. The background is that in 1995 not a single African-Caribbean boy at this school achieved five GCSE grades at A*–C. But in 1996 the proportion was 12 per cent. In 1997, it rose to 19 per cent. These percentages are still substantially below the national average so there is certainly no room for complacency. The improvement, however, was dramatic. Researchers who studied the school closely for the Department for Education and Employment concluded that the reasons for the improvement lay in fundamental changes in the school's ethos and relationships. The quotations in Box 35 are taken from the DfEE report and show the main features of the changes which took place. The quotations are particularly striking if read in conjunction with the earlier sections of this book on youth identity (pages 18-20), and on classroom interaction (pages 2-5).

Stories and situations

The stories in Box 36 are useful triggers for discussion of major issues. At an inservice training session or as an agenda item for a working party, such stories have the following benefits:

* If used at the start of a course or meeting, they give participants reassurance that the programme ahead is going to be down-to-earth and that it is likely to help them solve or manage the practical problems of their everyday work.

* They provide a useful reminder that even the best prepared plans can go wrong, and that unforeseen problems often arise. Successful change in education, as in other areas of work, requires among other things that there should be frank acknowledgement of uncertainties and failures, and hard-nosed anticipation of resistance and difficulty.

* They provide pegs on which to hang theoretical discussion, and thus they make communication easier. They can be referred to formally, for example in talks and lectures, and also in conversation.

* By omitting much basic detail, they invite discussion of underlying issues and causes, and of long-term plans for substantial institutional change.

* They encode challenging ideas and arguments, and in this way make them less threatening. All the stories in Box 36, in one way or another, are about institutional racism.

* They invite attention to the ways in which they themselves are constructed and narrated. Has the person telling the story misunderstood his or her situation? How might a different person narrate the same episode?

Box 35

Successful relationships – a case-study

Almost a third of the students at this school are African-Caribbean. In 1995 not a single African-Caribbean boy achieved five GCSE grades at A*–C. But in 1996 the proportion was 12 per cent. In 1997, it rose to 19 per cent. The reasons for this dramatic improvement, in the view of researchers who studied the school closely for the Department for Education and Employment, lay in fundamental changes in the school's ethos and relationships. The following quotations show the main features of these changes.

'The key to good relations in our school is that we take time to listen to the students. We give them a fair hearing. If students feel that you will listen to them and investigate things properly, and sometimes you spend a lot of time listening to something that you knew all the time, but the bottom line is, they know you will listen to them.'
– *deputy head*

'There has been a change in the way they handle Black kids here. The school has gone through a vast learning process With the influence of [the head], the teachers have become more educated about the ways of the Black children.'
– *a Black parent*

'Parents are able to come and talk to the head about their children getting arrested or getting into trouble outside the school. Parents have the confidence to come to her as a friend – she is seen as a friend in arms, struggling together with them for the good of their children.' – *a Black parent-governor*

'Black students are very aware of discrimination in the outside world. Many of them have experiences of unemployment, poverty, drugs, so that for some of them street cred is all they've got. Teachers in general are not tuned in to these problems. Instead, they feel threatened and afraid, so they send pupils out of class for trivial things ... Many teachers say that they care for all their students. But there is caring, and there is wanting to make a difference. At this school, the staff try to make a difference.' – *a teacher*

'The head has a good understanding of the needs of Black students, particularly boys. She tries to see where they are coming from and uses strategies to reduce conflict, and talks through with them about using strategies which reduce conflict with teachers ... She treats them as young adults rather than naughty children, and gives them equal treatment, recognising that she cannot treat all students the same because of different experiences. She doesn't automatically take the side of either the teacher or the pupil, but she is able to see the pupil's point of view.' – *chair of governors*

'We started working through individuals to reverse the trend among boys which says that to be an achiever is not cool. S., for example, he was able to be popular, to work and still have credibility with the other students. He didn't mind having his work pinned up. We have lads like that who don't mind having their work pinned up or who don't mind being highlighted. One of S's friends came in and asked for extra work at KS3 because he wanted to do as well as S.'
– *a teacher*

'... G. can be one of the lads and had slackened off a bit. He is a very bright boy but became more involved in the social side of life and was underachieving. So I called him and told him that he was becoming the equivalent of a 'dumb blonde' – tall and good looking but with nothing. He's very popular with the girls. I asked him if there was a particular girl that he liked and he said, 'E.'. So I said, 'She's not going to want you if you are not going to be of similar academic status. Your good looks aren't going to last for ever. You can't get through on that charm and smile. The kind of girls you like are not going to be interested if you're on the dole.' He knew exactly what I meant. He didn't like to be compared to a dumb blonde. Now he's one of our role models and we have great hopes of him.' – *the headteacher*

Source: *Making the Difference: teaching and learning strategies in successful multi-ethnic schools,* by Maud Blair and Jill Bourne et al for the Department for Education and Employment, 1998.

Box 36

What next? – stories and situations

Hysterical?

I'm a parent governor at my son's school. Another parent said to me the other day: 'Some of the staff, you know, they're like a pack of wolves, they're hunting our children down, they won't rest till they've got them expelled. And it's no coincidence that the staff who are doing this are all White and the kids they've got it in for are all Black.' I mentioned this to the head. 'The allegation is hysterical,' she said. 'It's wholly unfounded and unfair.'

What next?

I'm a Year 9 student. This week I wrote a poem in English about slavery. 'It's well expressed,' said the teacher, who's White, 'but terribly extreme. You don't really feel like that, do you?' – 'Of course I do,' I said. 'We all do. I'm angry about what you people did to us, and you're still doing it.' – 'It wasn't me that did it,' snapped the teacher, raising her voice, 'and any way I don't like the way you're talking to me about this.' And that was that. What next?

British

Last week we had an assembly on Martin Luther King's birthday. A school governor who was present commented afterwards: 'This is Britain, don't you think you should be teaching the children to be British? And what about our own English children? They're losing their identity, they don't know who they are, they have nothing to be proud of.' I didn't have a chance to reply. This week the governor has a letter in the local press saying the same things.

Biggest problem

An Ofsted inspector visiting the school the other day said the biggest problem facing British education today is poor attainment amongst White working class boys. 'You could also say,' remarked a colleague, who is incidentally a Black woman, 'that a major problem is the high level of racism, sexism and homophobia amongst such boys.' – 'So you think political correctness is more important than raising standards?' said the inspector. 'I strongly advise you, young lady, to change your views'.

Three or four years ago

I work for a race equality council and often have to deal with exclusions from schools. This week I went with a parent to see a headteacher. 'I'm sorry,' she said, 'but the situation's entirely impossible, we're totally at the end of the road. If only you had come three or four years ago, when he first started getting into trouble, we might have been able between us to turn him round.' – 'You're virtually sentencing him,' I said, 'to a lifetime in prison. – 'I know,' she said, 'but all the same he's got to leave this school'.

Box 36 continued

My direction

As an education welfare officer I had occasion this week to be in the staffroom at a local school. There was some discussion of the Stephen Lawrence inquiry. Suddenly someone said: 'These race relations do-gooders, they're off the wall, they have no idea what it's like being a teacher these days. League tables, the National Curriculum, and pupils who challenge, question, argue, flaunt their sexuality, flaunt their strength. I've had it up to here.' Silence. Everyone seemed to look in my direction, to hear what I would say.

Where was she?

A fight broke out today in the classroom of a young colleague still in his first year of teaching. It was the first lesson after lunch and the fight had in fact started in the playground. The two students were sent to the head of year, who sent them to the head, who sent them home. But where was the head when the fight started? Sitting in her office, that's what, which is how she seems to spend every lunchtime.

Sort this out ourselves

Two boys had been fighting in the playground, and had been separated by others. They were still shouting at each other when I arrived, and were both threatening to bring in knives the next day. 'And you keep out of this, you White bitch,' one of them said to me, 'this is nothing to do with you, we're going to sort this out ourselves'. He turned to the other boy. 'You gotta learn respect,' he said.

Challenge

One of the biggest problems at our school, I feel, is the approach to discipline of some of my male colleagues. They seem to treat every episode as a challenge to their own virility. They try to control the kids through their sheer physical presence, squaring up to them, standing up close to them, and shouting at them if they don't get their way. Many other colleagues seem to collude with this rather than question or criticise. Am I being too sensitive? Am I right to wish we could at least talk about this at an inset session?

Source: developed from inset material used at a London school, 1990s

Vicious and virtuous circles

Box 37 contains descriptions of episodes and issues which occur in classrooms, in relationships between teachers and pupils. Such episodes can be discussed and analysed – by pupils themselves as well as by staff at meetings and inset sessions – using a simple scheme sometimes known as 'ABC'. While all human behaviour is essentially interactive and highly complex, it is often possible to delineate a simple structure or pattern. For every behaviour (B) there are one or more antecedents (A) and one or more consequences (C). Similarly, several different pieces of behaviour may have a single significant antecedent and several different behaviours may have a single significant consequence. It is important to bear in mind, when using this scheme to analyse and discuss episodes and situations such as those in Boxes 36 and 37, that:

- '**A**' is not always in the immediate past: there may on the contrary be a long history of apparently insignificant behaviours; or A may be an attitude or world-view which has been developed over a lifetime's experience and is not directly related to the person(s) with whom the subject in question is currently interacting.

- '**B**' is not always a specific action: it might take the form of facial expression, stance, tone of voice, volume of speech, silence, non-compliance or actual or perceived attitude.

- '**C**' is not always in the immediate future: it may have a ripple effect and not be detected in behaviour for some time to come.

Strategies

In all interpersonal exchanges – not least in inter-cultural exchanges – an A-B-C cycle can be detected, whereby the consequence of one piece of behaviour becomes the antecedent for an another. (In algebraic terms, the C of B1 becomes an A of B2 and so on.) The significant question is: is it a vicious circle or a virtuous circle?

In schools this A-B-C structure is helpful:

- for staff in understanding both their own and their pupils' behaviours

- as a strategy for helping pupils to understand both their own and teachers' behaviour

- as a strategy which pupils can use throughout their lives in interaction with others.

Box 37

Classroom management situations

Situation 1

I teach a secondary class several times a week. Most of the time they are receptive to learning and there are no major problems with their behaviour. However, once a week, they come to me in a somewhat negative frame of mind: they seem variously bored or agitated, and I sense that often there are troubles brewing.

Situation 2

One pupil in a class I teach is persistently badly behaved, always showing off or otherwise seeking attention, it seems, and not doing well academically at all. Whenever I say something like, "If you worked harder and stopped messing around, you'd get on a lot better", it only makes things worse.

Situation 3

I teach a lively class with several strong personalities. One pupil is very quiet and self-contained, and seems a bit sad. The pupil gets on well with written work, does homework on time and is always cooperative - except when it comes to joining in group activities. The pupil doesn't participate in discussions, either.

Situation 4

I dread teaching one particular class and I can feel myself getting tense each time the lesson starts. There are several influential trouble makers and they are very rude to you: the other pupils find this very amusing and egg them on. No one seems to get anything done and noise levels are unacceptably high.

Situation 5

I teach a mixed ability class and group pupils by attainment to use certain materials or to engage in particular tasks or activities. One group in the class does not cooperate with each other at all: they won't share resources fairly, pool their ideas in an investigation or help each other out.

Situation 6

There are several pupils in a class I teach who are always at each others' throats. I usually manage to contain the situation by pouring oil on troubled waters and by trying to keep them sweet by not being too demanding. But now a 'slanging match' has just broken out and two pupils have come to blows.

Box 38

Avoiding destructive conflict – advice and warnings

1 Listen

Listen carefully when others speak. Also, 'listen out' – attend to the messages, feelings and concerns *behind* what they actually say, use your antennae, your intuition. Show you're listening (a) by not interrupting and (b) by reflecting back what the other says and asking if that's what they meant.

2 Think twice before offering advice or criticism

Be aware that unsolicited advice or criticism may come over as judgmental and aggressive, and may provoke a defensive or aggressive response.

3 Respect personal space

If you stand unusually close to someone, or pick up or touch their personal possessions without asking them, they may find this challenging and threatening, and react with anxiety or anger.

4 Danger signals

Be aware of your own feelings when you're getting anxious and angry, and think twice ('count up to ten') before expressing anger. Watch for danger signs in others, for example a raised voice, angry eyes, threatening gestures, which may indicate that they are about to lose their temper, and try not to be provocative.

5 Using friendly gestures

A wagging or pointing finger is threatening and provocative. Open hands with upturned palms indicate openness and trust.

6 Dragging up the past

Reminding someone of previous occasions when they have displeased you is often tempting. But don't be surprised if they react with anger.

7 History and hearsay

Don't rake over the past – but also, don't forget history. Every encounter between human beings takes place within a historical context, in the sense that everyone brings with them memories and expectations derived from previous experiences or from hearsay. Your own words and actions may well be entirely reasonable, from your own point of view. But someone else may interpret them differently, if they have memories and an outlook very different from yours.

8 Don't widen the scope

If you criticise other people as well as the person you're speaking to – 'you and your sort', 'people like you', 'you lot are all the same', 'you're as bad as your brother' – you will inevitably seem to be deliberately raising the stakes. For now the other person has to defend their family, friends and community – people they care about and feel loyalty to, and derive their core identity from – as well as themselves.

9 Giving reasons

An order, instruction or request on its own often comes over as abrupt and disrespectful. Explaining why you want something implies respect for the other person's capacity for reasoning and empathy.

10 Avoiding accusations

Accusations are inherently threatening, and may provoke an aggressive or defensive response. If you do wish to accuse, be sure of your ground. But don't be surprised if the other person takes offence.

11 Avoiding generalisations

'You're always...', 'you never ...', 'why can't you ever ...', are sure-fire ways of getting someone nettled, and making it likely that they will respond with anger or nurse resentment.

12 Permitting dignity

If you rebuke, criticise or ridicule someone in front of others, particularly people whose good opinion they value, they will feel humiliated. If you criticise in private they will not lose face, but will retain their dignity.

Source: some of the items in this list are derived from Tony Sewell's *Black Masculinities*, 1997, pages 211-12. Full details on page 85.

Avoiding destructive conflict

Box 38 contains 12 simple points about defusing conflict. When an argument in the playground escalates into a fight, it is probably because some of the simple suggestions or warnings in Box 38 have been neglected. The points can be taught to, discussed with and practised (for example in role-play) by pupils of all ages. The points are also relevant to relationships between pupils and teachers, in two separate ways:

If pupils want to avoid escalating disagreements with teachers to the point where they get into trouble, they need to be able to use the skills itemised in Box 38.

Similarly if teachers wish to avoid destructive confrontations with pupils, the points in Box 38 – even though embarrassingly obvious! – are all worth bearing in mind.

The points can also all be considered in relation to the classroom management situations listed in Box 37.

Working with parents and carers

Box 41, on page 60, contains a list of questions for self-review. It is also valuable to collect the impressions and perceptions of parents themselves.

The listening school

The most successful multi-ethnic schools, according to the research by Maud Blair and Jill Bourne and their colleagues for the Department for Education and Employment, published in 1998, were 'listening schools' – 'they took time to talk with students and parents' and 'were prepared to consider and debate values as well as strategies'. There is a fuller extract from the report in Box 39. One way of listening is through asking pupils to fill in questionnaires about their perceptions and feelings, or to discuss such questionnaires within the context of, for example, Personal, Social and Health Education (PSHE) lessons. A specimen questionnaire is provided in Box 40.

Box 39

'They took time to listen'

'The most effective schools were 'listening schools': schools which took time to talk with students and parents; which were prepared to consider and debate values as well as strategies; which took seriously the views students and parents offered and their own interpretations of school processes; and which used this learning to re-appraise, and where necessary change, their practices and to build a more inclusive curriculum.'

From *Making the Difference: teaching and learning strategies in successful multi-ethnic schools* by Maud Blair and Jill Bourne, Department for Education and Employment, 1998.

Like you're talking to me now

Josiah (not his real name) has been permanently excluded from three different primary schools, and arrived last week in Year 7 of a secondary school. A teacher happened to record a conversation with him. Part of it went as follows:

Teacher Did you feel they respected you at that school?

Josiah No

Teacher Can you tell me why?

Josiah They threw me out.

Teacher What about here, how can we help you here?

Josiah I want to be here, all my friends are here.

Teacher What about the teachers, how can we help you to stay?

Josiah I don't know.

Teacher How would you like us to treat you?

Josiah Be nice.

Teacher How would we talk to you if we were being nice?

Josiah Like you're talking to me now.

Source: submission from a London secondary school in connection with this book

Box 40

Feelings about school – a questionnaire

The purpose of this questionnaire is to find out how you feel about school. It consists of a series of statements. For each statement please put a tick in one of the columns, to show your view.

	Strongly disagree	Partly disagree	Not sure	Partly agree	Strongly agree
There's at least one teacher here who cares about me.	☐	☐	☐	☐	☐
By and large the teachers seem to like me.	☐	☐	☐	☐	☐
I feel I'm making good progress at this school.	☐	☐	☐	☐	☐
I enjoy learning.	☐	☐	☐	☐	☐
I expect to do well.	☐	☐	☐	☐	☐
I get given a lot of responsibility.	☐	☐	☐	☐	☐
The teachers seem to expect the best of me.	☐	☐	☐	☐	☐
I have generally been treated fairly by the school.	☐	☐	☐	☐	☐
The school shows respect for students of all races and cultures.	☐	☐	☐	☐	☐
I have never been bullied or insulted because of my race or culture.	☐	☐	☐	☐	☐
The school takes a strong stand against racism.	☐	☐	☐	☐	☐
Most lessons are interesting.	☐	☐	☐	☐	☐
The school is a good place for boys.	☐	☐	☐	☐	☐
The school is a good place for girls.	☐	☐	☐	☐	☐
The teachers give me respect.	☐	☐	☐	☐	☐

There is no need to give your name. But do please show your gender, the year you're in and your culture or race (eg Black, Asian, African, Caribbean, White – write whatever word best describes you.)

Gender: male/female   Year: Race or culture:

Let no one or no circumstances render you less that you are, or less
than you know you have the capacity to be
– **Gus John**, talking about *Windrush*, 1998

Box 41

Working with parents and carers – questions for review

Do we take measures to ensure that Black parents are proportionately as involved as other parents in activities such as:

- representation on the governing body?
- assistance in classrooms and on outings?
- attendance at parents evenings?
- fundraising?
- careers guidance?
- use of special facilities for parents?
- the development of profiles and records of achievement?
- support for home reading and home mathematics schemes?

Are the school's arrangements for receiving and welcoming visitors appropriate and accessible for parents and carers of all backgrounds?

Is information material for parents and potential parents reader-friendly, and is available in languages other than English as appropriate?

Are parents, carers and members of the local community frequently involved in the curriculum, for example by:

- giving talks
- contributing to storytelling and oral history projects
- providing classroom support
- assisting with careers guidance?

At occasions such as evenings for parents and carers, are interpreters available as appropriate?

Do we have a special room for parents to use?

Do we ensure that we send letters to individual parents about their children's successes and achievements?

Does a senior member of staff have specific responsibility for reviewing and improving relationships and contacts with parents?

When relationships break down – permanent exclusion from school

During the 1990s there was a massive rise in the number of pupils and students excluded permanently from school. There was a massive rise also – though this is less well documented nationally with precise figures – in the use of fixed-term exclusions. Why? What can be done about it? Why are African Caribbean young people, both girls and boys, disproportionately affected? What can be done to reduce and remove differentials in the exclusion rates of pupils and students from different ethnic backgrounds? These are the questions raised and discussed in the pages which follow.

The facts and points in these pages are taken from papers published in 1998 by the Social Exclusion Unit and the London Research Centre, and from a range of academic articles and reports published in the 1990s. (See page 84 for detailed references.)

The chapter then continues with notes and reminders of things an individual school can do to improve relationships and to cut down on exclusions and improve relationships (Box 44). Throughout the chapter there are references to ways in which conflicts and disputes between teachers and pupils can be defused or prevented. This whole issue of conflict prevention and resolution is considered in further detail in Box 38.

School exclusion and social exclusion

There is a two-way link between school exclusion and social exclusion. On the one hand, young people excluded from school are more likely to be unemployed after the age of 16, not least because they do not obtain adequate qualifications, and are more likely to become involved in crime. On the other, it is mainly young people from families and households which are already suffering from social exclusion (unemployment, poverty, poor housing, poor health) who are at risk of being excluded from school. The two kinds of exclusion – school and social – are a vicious circle: each is for the other both the chicken and the egg.

What are the general underlying causes?

This is a matter of speculation and controversy. The following arguments are frequently advanced:

(1) Increasing inequality in wider society has put additional stress on the households most disadvantaged by poverty. Children and young people from such households pose additional and more challenging problems for schools. In particular they are more inclined to engage in acts of violence or disruption. (The most recent government research, published in March 1999, shows that two in five of all children are born in families defined as poor. The definition of a household in poverty is one whose income is less than half the national average. The definition is therefore about relative poverty, i.e. inequality, rather than absolute poverty.)

(2) The national curriculum and assessment arrangements make it more difficult than previously for schools to provide an inclusive curriculum, and more difficult to provide sound programmes of personal and social education. Further, schools no longer have resources to provide the personal one-to-one attention which the most disaffected and 'difficult' young people need.

(3) Changes in education since 1988 have made schools anxious about their place in league tables and about their reputation in the local community. In consequence they have a lower tolerance than previously of non-conforming behaviour.

It is also sometimes suggested that there has been a rise in bad behaviour in schools due to a rise in the so-called 'yob culture' among young men. Against this it may be pointed out that a proportion of young working class men have always been disaffected by schooling, and that current concerns about them are a kind of moral panic, connected with economic changes which have reduced the availability of unskilled or semi-skilled jobs for male workers, rather than responses to something new in young people themselves.

Who is most at risk?

Young people in the following categories are more likely than others to experience exclusion from school:

1. boys

2. in years 9,10 and 11 at secondary school

3. victims of social deprivation, as measured by entitlement to free school meals

4. having special educational needs

5. being looked after by local authorities

6. living in London

7. of African Caribbean or mixed Caribbean and White heritage. The latest DfEE figures show that the exclusion rate nationally amongst African Caribbeans (6.6 per thousand) is three times the rate for White pupils (1.8 per 1,000). In some parts of England there has been a rise in recent years in the number of exclusions of young people from Pakistani and Bangladeshi backgrounds.

What specific causes underlie the exclusion of African Caribbean young men?

First, it must be recognised that the statistics currently available do not compare like with like, since they do not take into account the variable of social disadvantage. If social disadvantage and exclusion are factors associated with exclusion from school, as they appear to be, and if African Caribbean households suffer disproportionately from social disadvantage (which they do, particularly in employment and income), then disproportionate experience of exclusion from school is not statistically surprising – even though it is humanly distressing and most certainly in need of urgent attention.

Another factor which may skew the statistics is more speculative but worth mentioning. It is that White boys at risk of exclusion are more likely than Black boys to play truant. In other words they exclude themselves from school before they get into serious trouble. They are in consequence severely disadvantaged, but do not show up in the statistics for exclusions. This speculation needs to be researched, so it can be either confirmed or refuted.

Box 42

Reducing exclusions – one school's story

About a quarter of the students at Lodge High School (not its real name) are Black. Three years ago, Black students at Lodge High were 7.8 times more likely to be permanently excluded than White students – i.e. the proportion of Black students who were excluded was almost eight times the proportion of White students who were excluded. In liaison with the LEA, the school set up a three-year project whose twin aims were (a) to cut drastically the school's use of both fixed-term and permanent exclusions and (b) to reduce to nil, if possible, the differential between Black and White. Both aims were achieved. By the end of the second year of the project, the differential had dropped from 7.8 to 4.6. In the third year, the differential wholly disappeared, to the point where in fact Black students were less likely than White (though the raw figures were too low to be statistically significant) to experience permanent exclusion.

In order to cut down on exclusions generally, the staff reviewed the kinds of offence which most often led to exclusion – defined in the records mainly as 'defiance', 'disruption', 'disobedience', 'non-compliance with the school's behaviour code', and not turning up for detentions. Heads of year took a policy decision to use exclusion much less for these kinds of offence, and developed both in themselves and in colleagues the skills of responding to 'defiance', etc, in ways which defused conflict rather than exacerbated it.

Specifically to improve the behaviour of Black students, the school introduced a mentoring scheme. This involved the appointment of a full-time co-ordinator using Section 11 funding in liaison with the LEA, and considerable attention to – and resourcing of – efficient management and administration. In Box 43 there are quotations from both mentors and students. They show vividly the main kinds of benefit which well-run mentoring schemes can have for everyone directly involved in them. In addition, such schemes have many indirect benefits for the general ethos and curriculum of the schools where they are based.

Source: documents submitted for the compilation of this book.

Box 43

A mentoring scheme – views and responses

At the end of the school year, both pupils and mentors were asked to write their reflections. Here are some of the points they made:

Reflections by pupils

'I am now more organised and plan things in advance. eg packing my bag the night before.'

'I needed to join the scheme because I got excluded several times because of my behaviour and attitude. I have achieved not a lot but I'm working on it. My mentor says there's lots of room for improvement.'

'I can now be good in lessons. I haven't been on report. I have not been sent out of the lesson. I have learnt to be patient when the teacher is talking and not be distracted by my friends. I haven't been in a fight.'

'I have changed quite a lot since joining the mentor scheme. I don't get in trouble as much as I used to.'

'I feel good talking with my mentor because he understands me.'

'Much better at reading and writing.'

'I express my feelings and know who I am and how I feel.'

Reflections by mentors

'D's poem shows positive evidence of his intentions and commitment to a fruitful existence at school. He portrays a realisation of the link between education and all-round success for the black student in this country.'

'In a counselling role I have facilitated exploration by my mentee of the barriers to his achievement. This honesty has enabled him to identify strategies that will assist him, and although he is not always able to adopt them things have certainly improved.'

'My mentee is beginning to have a different perspective on life. It is a long slow process ... Given time, my mentee could be a role model herself.'

'The scheme has highlighted the benefits of having a role-model for young people. In some way or another we all have them, whether parents, brothers, sisters or television personalities. I am glad I have used my position to be of some influence and sometimes change T's way of thinking.'

Source: from documents submitted for the compilation of this book

The fact remains that African Caribbean young men are considerably more at risk of exclusion than other young men. Even more seriously, since vastly greater numbers are involved, they are at risk of leaving school with poor or worthless paper qualifications, and therefore with lamentably poor life-chances.

What is the cause of this? The argument in this book is that schools and individual teachers see and treat African Caribbean young men differently, and less favourably, than other pupils. This is seldom due to conscious racism, but is almost certainly related to the kinds of unconscious and institutional racism that the Stephen Lawrence inquiry revealed in the police service. The inquiry defined institutional racism as 'the collective failure of an organisation to provide an appropriate professional service'. It added that such racism can 'be seen or detected' in attitudes as well as in processes and behaviour, and that discrimination and disadvantage can be the consequence of 'unwitting prejudice, ignorance, thoughtlessness and racist stereotyping'. There are fuller notes on the concept of institutional racism in Boxes 22 and 23 on pages 32 and 34.

In the background, so to speak, of institutional racism in schools, there is institutional racism in wider society – the ways in which organisations disadvantage and exclude Black and other minority people, and therefore serve to perpetuate inequalities in employment, health, well-being and influence. This wider context affects both schools on the one hand and young Black men on the other.

Specific reasons for exclusions

Different schools and local authorities record the reasons for exclusion in a range of different ways. It is therefore difficult to generalise from the statistics which are available. However, the overall pattern is that the most common reasons given for excluding a pupil are to do with (a) disruption, disobedience or defiance or (b) violence amongst pupils. Assaults on staff and serious criminal offences (stealing, bullying younger pupils, or carrying weapons or drugs) are relatively rare, though they sometimes feature prominently in media reporting. The differences between different ethnic groups appear to be small or non-existent. (But each school needs to make its own analysis in this respect. It may happen that in some schools Black pupils and White are excluded for different kinds of offence. Many Black parents and

community leaders believe that schools treat 'defiance' or 'disobedience' by Black pupils more punitively than the same behaviour by White pupils.)

Consequently, most of the measures taken to reduce the number of exclusions need to focus (a) on preventing disruption and disobedience, or on dealing with disruption and disobedience in ways which defuse and de-escalate tensions rather than exacerbate them, and (b) on addressing directly the propensity of some pupils to resort to violence when 'settling' disputes amongst themselves. In both these respects, it is relevant to consider the points in Box 38 on page 57. The points are relevant for defusing confrontations between teachers and pupils as well as for managing conflict amongst pupils in the playground and on the street.

Action at various levels

An individual school can do a great deal to cut down on exclusions. However, it will almost certainly need substantial support, including financial support, from its LEA. Local authorities, for their part, may need substantial support from central government.

Action at school level to reduce exclusions

The list in Box 44 is based on recommendations published by, amongst others, the Commission for Racial Equality, the Department for Education and Employment, the Runnymede Trust, the Social Exclusion Unit and the Working Group Against Racism in Children's Resources. The research basis for the recommendations derives from recent work at the University of Birmingham, University of Nottingham, Nottingham Trent University and the Open University. There are full references on page 85.

Several of the items on the list have clear implications for LEAs. It cannot be over-emphasised that a concerted approach to reducing exclusions has to be made, and that action at any one level is unlikely to be sufficient if it is not complemented, supported and reinforced by action at other levels also.

Box 44

Action by schools to improve relationships

Explicit prioritising

State clearly in the school development plan that the school intends (a) to cut down on exclusions (both permanent and fixed-term) of all pupils and (b) to reduce and remove any differential between exclusion rates for pupils of different ethnic backgrounds. Include relevant data on last three years and numerical targets for the next three years.

Monitoring and records

Ensure that data is kept by ethnicity, gender, special educational needs, socio-economic background (for example by entitlement to free school meals) on both permanent and fixed-term exclusions, and on reasons for exclusion. (Also, note any patterns in relation to which teachers are most frequently involved, which curriculum subjects, what times of the day and week when incidents take place, and so on.) Obtain information on such patterns in other similar schools, and make comparisons.

Additional and specialist staffing

Appoint or use additional staffing (eg trained mediation workers, counsellors, school-community liaison workers) to help deal with specific problems which arise; to work with individual pupils at risk of exclusion (fixed-term as well as permanent); to act as advocates and mediators; and to contribute to staff training and awareness. Ensure such staff have sufficient status and influence, and that they are supported with ongoing training and with opportunities to meet and reflect with colleagues doing similar work in other schools.

Mentoring

Ensure that pupils at risk of exclusion have a personal mentor. The most successful mentoring schemes have most or all of the following factors in common: (a) mentors are drawn from a range of occupational backgrounds; (b) they are ethnically matched, where possible, with their mentees (c) they receive training, encouragement and support (d) there is sufficient investment in resources for administration and management (d) the mentors are trusted to respect confidentiality but also, if requested, to act as mediators, representatives or advocates in any disputes which arise (e) mentors visit lessons (f) there is a strong focus on academic work as well as on personal and social development (g) the scheme is well integrated with the mainstream activities and structures of the school. There are fuller details about a successful mentoring scheme in Boxes 42 and 43.

Contact with supplementary schools

Establish and maintain good links with supplementary schools and Saturday schools attended by pupils. For example, involve staff from supplementary provision as tutors and speakers in staff training; invite them to school events; send representatives to events organised by supplementary schools; ensure that class teachers or form tutors are aware of their pupils' involvement in supplementary provision; seek advice and assistance in relation to specific issues.

Interaction as equals

Ensure that White staff are able to listen to the experiences and perceptions of Black people. Too many White people only meet Black people within contexts where they are the ones who have formal authority – within the context of teacher-pupil relationships, for example, or in teacher-parent contacts. They therefore need to meet and interact with Black people in situations where there is formal equality, for example in working parties which contain at least as many Black people as White, and in situations where it is Black people rather than White who have formal authority.

Cooling-off area

As part of a programme to help pupils deal with anger and stress, provide a sanctuary within the school for pupils who need a cooling-off period when they are stressed or angry, and maybe seething with 'school rage'. Avoid using this as a 'sin bin' to which pupils are sent as a punishment. Sometimes a pupil needs to be with a specific teacher or counsellor rather than in a special place. It is frequently valuable to provide expert counselling assistance, as for example in 'The Place To Be' project, described in Box 45.

Box 44 continued

Discipline policy

Review the official behaviour policy to ensure that it (a) states that permanent exclusion will only ever be used as a last resort (b) indicates that few if any offences automatically carry a tariff of fixed-term exclusion (c) contains a code of practice indicating how staff are expected to behave towards pupils.

Appeals procedures

Ensure that (a) pupils are represented by an advocate, preferably with specialist training, knowledge and expertise (b) at least one member of the appeals panel is of the same ethnic background as the pupil threatened with exclusion (c) evidence presented to the panel will be relevant to a specific offence, not in the form of a dossier or file referring to a lengthy period.

Primary/secondary transfer

Review arrangements for transfer to secondary school, to reduce to a minimum the possibility of disaffection and alienation arising at this time. Pay particular attention at this time to the likelihood that certain pupils will have negative experiences, and that they may react by turning against the school's norms and expectations.

Complaints and grievances

Set up systems whereby pupils can complain when they feel they have been treated unfairly by a teacher. Also, make it permissible for a pupil to be accompanied by a friend, if they wish, when they are in trouble with a teacher.

Avoiding escalation of conflict

Ensure that as many staff as possible receive training in ways of defusing and resolving conflict, including conflict between themselves and pupils as well as conflict between pupils (fuller information in Box 38).

Peer mediation schemes

Train students and pupils themselves in skills and techniques of reducing, defusing and resolving conflict.

Inclusive curriculum

Review all subject areas, to ensure that they take opportunities to recognise and respect pupils' cultural and ethnic identities. (See chapter 4 for substantial detail.)

Special Educational Needs

Review assessment procedures to ensure that pupils with behavioural and learning difficulties are correctly identified at the earliest possible time, and that appropriate additional support is (a) secured and (b) provided.

Direct teaching

Include direct teaching about behaviour and behaviour management in, for example, PSHE programmes. Teach, for instance, the differences between 'assertive', 'aggressive' and 'submissive' behaviour, using role-play, stories, case-studies, discussion, etc. And use the simple ABC scheme ('antecedents', 'behaviour', 'consequences') described in this book on page 56 to analyse and discuss things which happen in classrooms and the playground.

Discussion and collaboration skills

In all curriculum subjects teach and practise discussion skills – listening, talking reflectively and exploratively, summarising, affirming others, taking turns, keeping to the point, using examples and anecdotes sensitively, and so on – and the skills required for collaborating within a small group.

Induction and reintegration

Obtain additional resources to support the induction and integration of pupils and students admitted to the school who have been excluded from other schools.

Reintegration after fixed-term exclusions

Ensure that there is a carefully thought-out programme for reintegrating pupils who return to school after a fixed-term exclusion.

Box 45

The Place To Be

'Three years ago my teachers were feeling got at from all sides because of the pressure of SATs, league tables and national curriculum requirements. Exclusions seemed the obvious answer because it is easier to teach without difficult children in class ... Significantly our school, like other schools that have adopted The Place To Be model, have found exclusions have dropped to nil.' – *headteacher of a primary school in London.*

'The Place To Be is not a good cause but a practical matter of necessity concerning the mental health of young children. If a child doesn't have emotional support at school there isn't any hope of them achieving their potential ... As well as providing a safe place where children can think and explore their feelings, the outcome is they're far more settled, feel better about themselves and can go back into the classroom to learn.' – *director of The Place To Be.*

Information from: The Place To Be, Edinburgh House, 154-182 Kennington Lane, London SE11 4EZ.

Peer mediation

Mediation Works is a valuable manual for secondary schools, with detailed guidance on setting up peer mediation services within individual schools. Available from Mediation UK, Alexander House, Telephone Avenue, Bristol BS1 4BS.

6. PROJECTS

This chapter welcomes the new Ethnic Minority Achievement
Grant (EMAG), and provides case-study descriptions of
two projects – one in a primary school about English
as an additional language, the other in a secondary school
about African-Caribbean achievement – which EMAG
could be used to fund. The chapter also contains some notes
on national and local formulas for allocating the new grant.

Headings in this chapter

Boxes in this chapter

Welcome to new source of funds

In principle, the new Ethnic Minority Achievement Grant (EMAG) has many advantages over the scheme which it replaces, Section 11. These include:

- the central stress on *achievement*, not principally on acquiring English

- the requirement that *schools*, not LEAs, should accept basic responsibility for raising the achievement of all their pupils

- the stress on sound *statistics*, at both LEA and school-levels

- the emphasis on *training*, for both specialist and mainstream staff

- the acknowledgement that *traditional Section 11-type support teaching is not in itself sufficient* to raise achievement

- the stress that there is a need, in the words of the initial documentation about the grant from the DfEE, for '*innovative approaches* designed to achieve a step change in the achievement of minority ethnic pupils'

- the intention to allocate resources according to *objective measures of need*

- the requirement that both schools and LEAs should cooperate with *independent evaluations*

Principles of allocation

At the time that this book went to press it was not clear what the criteria would be for allocating the grant nationally between different LEAs, nor whether LEAs would be expected to allocate it to schools according to criteria drawn up centrally. It is reasonable to hope that both nationally and within each LEA formulas will be developed which recognise that:

- schools receiving refugee and asylum-seeking pupils need extra resources over and above those which they receive for pupils at early stages of English acquisition

- it takes at *least* five years for a pupil from another country to catch up with peers who have English as their native language

- the yardstick for comparisons when assessing achievement and under-achievement should be national averages, not LEA averages or school averages

- it is essential to focus not only on pupils for whom English is an additional language but also on under-achievement amongst Black pupils who are native and/or fluent speakers of English

- new formulas should use objective data, not professional judgement, in order that they may be accepted as fair by all interested parties

- new formulas should signal to schools how, in general terms, they are expected to use the resources they receive, and how their use of them will be monitored and evaluated.

Accountability

If EMAG is to be successful there will need to be partnerships involving:

- Black and other minority communities, at national, LEA and neighbourhood levels

- schools

- local authorities

- the DfEE

Each school, it follows, must be accountable both to its LEA and to its parents. Through Ofsted, each school must be accountable to the DfEE. Each LEA must be accountable in three separate directions: (a) its local voluntary sector (b) its schools (c) the DfEE. Crucially, the DfEE must be held accountable – to voluntary organisations nationally, to LEAs, and directly to schools.

Existing accountability structures must be fully used – governing bodies, LEA committees, Parliament. But also new, less formal but more flexible and responsive structures and forums need to be developed.

The DfEE has stated that the new grant will be subject to independent evaluation with which schools and LEAs will need to cooperate. It is to be hoped that the DfEE will seek and take advice from academics and community organisations on how in practice such independent evaluations should be conducted, and who will be involved in (a) clarifying and negotiating their procedures (b) scrutinising their outcomes (c) disseminating their findings and (d) monitoring the implementation of recommendations which are made on the basis of them.

Funding for whole-school change

Whatever allocation formula is used, it will send out important signals to schools. That is why formulas for the EMAG must be more sensitive than most formulas used in the past for Section 11.

However, even after 32 years of Section 11 there is little clarity or professional consensus nationally on what in practice needs to be done to support bilingual pupils at 'stage three' and 'stage four' of acquiring English, and even less clarity and professional consensus on what needs to be done to raise achievement among, for example, African-Caribbean pupils. There is a great need, it follows, for high-quality inservice training in the classroom-action-research mode for mainstream class and subject teachers, and for the additional teachers appointed under the auspices of EMAG.

One possible new approach would involve making an internal secondment of an experienced member of staff. Such a project is described in Box 48. Another possible approach would be a special project concerned with African-Caribbean achievement, for example a project such as the one described in Box 47.

Most Section 11-funded schemes in England in recent years have used the notion of 'targeted pupils' or 'focus pupils'. Each teacher has been responsible for monitoring and supporting the development of about 30 'targeted' pupils each term. The new EMAG scheme will almost certainly permit or encourage more flexible ways of using resources within a school. It would frequently be appropriate, for example, to 'target' or 'focus on' a whole class or year-group, and a particular aspect of pedagogy within a class or year-group – for example, collaborative groupwork, problem-solving, key visuals, writing frames – rather than individual pupils. Both of the projects described in Boxes 46 and 47 depart from the traditional notion of 'targeted pupils'. But both would be rigorously evaluated with regard to their impact on achievement.

Box 46

African-Caribbean Achievement Project

Summary

The African-Caribbean Achievement Project starts in 1999 at a secondary school in London. About a quarter of the school's students are of Caribbean heritage. The governors intend that it should run for a minimum of five years and hope that it will be funded by the Ethnic Minority Achievement Grant for its full duration. The aim is to close the differential between African-Caribbean achievement at the school and the national average. The project will act as a catalyst or change-agent, seeking over time to influence all major areas of school life to contribute to whole-school change and improvement. This preliminary briefing paper about the project has three main parts:

Part A   Structure and organisation

Part B   Issues to be addressed

Part C   Programme and activities

PART A: STRUCTURE AND ORGANISATION

1 Staffing

The school is appointing a full-time director. The salary-scale will be that of a Senior Teacher and the person appointed will be a member of the school's senior management team. He or she will have substantial experience of working with African-Caribbean students at secondary level, preferably in a supplementary school as well as in a mainstream school. In addition, there will be the equivalent each year of a .5 secondment of existing staff. In the first year, five staff will be seconded each for one day a week to work on specific aspects of the project and to integrate it with the work of their faculty, department or year-group.

2 Overall steering committee

The headteacher will chair a steering committee whose ten members will include five people from outside the school staff. The committee will act as a sounding-board to the director; will receive termly reports; will scrutinise proposals; and will approve the general lines of the project's policies and approaches. It will also be expected from time to time to engage in fund-raising, and to take part in other public activities relating to the project, and as individuals its members will give the director assistance reflecting their own specialist expertise and knowledge.

3 Student steering committee

A steering committee of students will similarly act as a sounding board, will receive reports and scrutinise proposals, will give assistance and moral support, and will be involved from time to time in fund-raising. Its members will be drawn from all parts of the school.

4 Support and consultancy

The director will have his or her own personal mentor or consultant, probably based at a university. There will be regular meetings with the mentor to review progress and to consider particular problems which have arisen, and in addition the mentor will be available on the telephone at times when the project's director needs advice or guidance on a specific point. In addition the director will be encouraged to be involved in appropriate professional networks where he or she can meet and interact with Black professionals involved in analogous work in other settings, and can exchange ideas and reflections.

5 Links and liaison within the school

Each department will nominate someone to act as contact person with the project.

6 Friends and supporters

The project will establish a constituency of friends and supporters – people who will be interested to be kept informed, and to give various kinds of assistance when requested. Such people will include parents and members of the local community, other staff at the school, teachers at other schools, and academics and activists with a specialist interest in the educational achievement of African-Caribbean young people. The project expects to send a termly newsletter to all its friends and supporters, and to invite them to occasional events such as conferences, seminars, exhibitions and open evenings.

7 Administration

The project's director will have his or her personal office and telephone line, and a capitation grant for resources.

PART B: ISSUES TO BE ADDRESSED

In broad terms the project expects to be concerned with the following topics:

- the content of the curriculum
- practical classroom pedagogy, including in particular problem-solving and collaborative groupwork
- relationships and conflict-resolution
- youth culture and personal identity
- parental involvement
- liaison with supplementary schools

Box 46 continued

PART C: PROGRAMME AND ACTIVITIES

It is as yet too early to state with certainty how the project will operate. The steering committee is still being formed, and the director has not yet been appointed. The exact programme of activities will depend on consultations and deliberations once the director has started work, and also – in the first instance – on the director's principal strengths and interests. It is expected that the project will initiate, manage or cooperate with activities such as the following:

1 Mentoring

Other schools have found that a well-organised mentoring scheme can be directly beneficial to all those involved in it, and has a valuable indirect influence on the school where it is based. (For further brief information see note 1.)

2 Black Studies

Courses in Black history and culture are valuable for developing students' self-esteem and self-confidence, and in providing a space where issues of immediate importance and relevance to Black students can be discussed and explored. Such courses can be free-standing outside the main curriculum, or can be modules within history or personal and social education. (Note 2.)

3 Primary/secondary transition

The months before and after a student starts at a new secondary school are critical for his or her feelings about school, and therefore for future success. They are critical also for parents. The project will look closely at ways in which this important time can be managed – for parents as well as for the pupils themselves – with maximum sensitivity and efficiency. (Note 3.)

4 Student support groups

Often Black students benefit from being able to talk among themselves, with facilitation and guidance by a sympathetic adult, about problems they are experiencing. (Note 4.)

5 Staff training

The project will almost certainly initiate and support staff training sessions, including sessions on conflict-resolution. It is recognised that staff need to be able to help students settle disputes without recourse to violence, and that they need skills in defusing disputes between themselves and students before these escalate into unproductive confrontations. (Note 5.)

6 Work and cooperation with parents

The project will probably set up and service a number of Black Parents Support Groups.

7 Liaison with supplementary schools

The project will tap into the expertise and experience of local supplementary schools, and also into the expertise of other agencies – including pupil referral units, Black-majority churches and youth and community provision – which have successful experience of working with Black youth.

8 Monitoring

The project will assist with the development of monitoring outcomes by ethnicity. This will involve, amongst other things, looking closely at attainment in different subjects, and identifying particular strengths and weaknesses. (Note 6.)

9 Classroom observation

The project will organise classroom observation activities in which senior staff give particular attention to the behaviour and motivation of Black students, and to the ways in which teachers interact with Black students. (Note 7.)

10 Classroom-action-research

The project will support classroom-action-research activities, geared in particular to developing problem-solving skills, discussion skills and collaboration skills. (Note 8.)

11 Peer mediation

The project will liaise closely with the school's new peer mediation programme. (Note 9.)

Notes

1   On mentoring, see the quotations in Box 43 and the reference to mentoring in Box 44.

2   The school cited in Box 35 found that a special course in Afrikan Studies was a valuable catalyst for change. A course in Black Studies is likely to include concepts of racism in its subject-matter (chapter 3), and tensions connected with youth and Black British identity (chapter 2 – see in particular Box 12 on street cred and school norms).

3   The critical importance of primary/secondary transition for Black students is mentioned in the 'Life and life-chances story', Box 5.

4   'Ursula', the girl quoted in Box 4, mentions the potential value of student support groups.

5   Issues and topics to be dealt with in conflict-resolution training are mentioned in Box 38.

6   On monitoring by ethnicity, see chapter 7, particularly Boxes 49 and 51.

7   On classroom management, see for example the story in Box 3 and the situations in Box 37.

8   On problem-solving and collaborative groupwork, see pages 44-47.

9   On peer-mediation, see the reference on page 66.

Source: papers and proposals developed at a school in London, 1999

Box 17

Secondments for whole-school change

Glowing terms

Midleigh School is a primary school with twelve staff. About half the pupils have learnt or are learning English as an additional language. An Ofsted inspection report recently praised the school in glowing terms, referring in particular to English and language development. It attributed the school's high standards in English largely to its involvement in a four-year Learning and Language Programme, now nearing completion.

Time and energy

For the whole of the first year of the project Midleigh's language coordinator, Aysha Malik, was taken off regular class teaching and she devoted all her time and energy to leading, developing and assisting her colleagues. In order that she could do this, she received considerable support from outside the school as well as from Midleigh's headteacher.

Course for change agents

Every Monday throughout the year Aysha was away from school on a course. The other course members were people very similar to herself – language coordinators in their respective schools. They were from several different LEAs, by the way. The course content had four separate aspects. First, there was great emphasis on **language**. Aysha and the other course members were intrigued and pleased by the new terms and ideas they encountered: 'semantic agility', 'rich scripting', 'key visual'. They extended their own enjoyment of the sounds, senses and powers of words. Second, there was much reference to **school effectiveness** and school improvement, and to the skills and strategies required of change agents such as Aysha herself, for example. Third, there was much stress on practical **classroom pedagogy**, including in particular problem-solving and collaborative groupwork. Fourth, there was quite a lot of **sociology** and political philosophy. Aysha was initially surprised and dismayed, but in the event pleased, when she had to write an extended essay entitled 'Inclusive Schools, Inclusive Society: why, what, where, how and when'. To prepare this she had to use concepts of racialisation and institutional racism, ethnogenesis and hybrid identity, cultural politics and postmodernism, and urban policy and regeneration.

Her own action-research

Not that theoretical essays were the principal kinds of written assignment on the course. Mainly the course members had to engage in classroom-action-research projects in their own schools. Aysha's own research was into children's imaging of word meanings in mathematics and into the use of texts with Year 4 children about inter-ethnic conflict and the negotiation of ethnic identity. The course tutor visited Aysha at her school at least once each term during the year, and met and talked at length with the headteacher as well as with Aysha herself. At the end of the year Aysha received the Advanced Diploma in Primary Language Education and credits towards the masters degree which, incidentally, she completed two years later.

Friends and critics

That was how Aysha spent her Mondays. On Tuesday mornings she visited other course members in their respective schools or in her turn received visits from others. The concept of critical friend was central to the course and it was on Tuesday mornings that course members developed and practised their skills as critics and friends, and the skills of receiving and acting on what their friends told them.

Colleagues

For five of the other seven sessions each week Aysha was involved in collaborative or partnership teaching with her colleagues. For two of them she acted in effect as a supply teacher so that colleagues could attend off-site ten-session courses. By the end of the year six different colleagues had attended such courses. Two of the courses were on linguistics and language development, the other four on specific curriculum areas – music, science, art and mathematics. All these courses had a clear central focus on the achievement of Black and other minority pupils.

Turns

That was the first year of the project. The following year Punita Gill, the head of infants, was released from regular class teaching and she operated in much the same way. This year it's the turn of Chris Webber, who is Midleigh School's maths coordinator. Next year it will be Pat Avery, who is taking over from Aysha as the school's language coordinator. Aysha herself, it so happens, will from next term be the school's new deputy head.

Standards

As already mentioned, the school received a glowing Ofsted report earlier this year, commenting in particular on children's high standards of literacy. An interim report from the School Effectiveness Research Unit at a nearby university has recorded objective quantifiable evidence that standards of English are considerably higher at Midleigh than at otherwise similar schools. The research also shows, intriguingly, that there has been less staff illness and turnover at Midleigh than at other similar schools these past three years, considerably less disruptive behaviour by pupils, and more and livelier parental involvement.

Source: a paper presented at a conference organised by the Schools Curriculum and Assessment Authority, 1995. The project was fictitious.

7. EVALUATION

This chapter considers how the various practical projects proposed
or recommended in previous chapters should be evaluated.
In particular it is concerned with the collection and analysis
of statistical data. It acknowledges and stresses also, however,
that qualitative data must be collected and acted on. It mentions in
this connection how earlier sections of this book can be used as
resources for evaluation and reflection. Evaluation has to take
place in each individual school, and be undertaken by teachers
and their pupils and their parents, as well as at LEA and
national levels, and must always be linked to practice and action.

Headings in this chapter

Boxes in this chapter

Monitoring by ethnicity

A report from Ofsted, *Raising the Attainment of Minority Ethnic Pupils*, published in March 1999, castigates schools and LEAs for not collecting and using ethnic statistics. 'A longstanding obstacle to progress,' it declares, 'is the reluctance of schools and LEAs to monitor pupil performance by ethnic group.' Its criticisms include also the following:

> Very few primary schools ... currently make effective use of the increasing amounts of data available to raise the attainment of minority ethnic pupils. (*Paragraph* 47)

> Many [secondary] schools have rich databases, but few use them to gain a coherent picture of the relative attainments by ethnicity of pupils entering in Year 7. (*Paragraph* 54)

> Even when schools receive good quality data [from their LEA] analysed by ethnicity, few make constructive use of it... In most cases the information remains unused. There is a need for further training and guidance on how to analyse and respond to such information. (*Paragraph* 49)

The report acknowledges (*Paragraph 216*) that central government itself has failed for many years to lead by example, and has failed even to require the collection of ethnically-based data, let alone to provide guidance or practical support. It was not until the introduction of the Ethnic Minority Achievement Grant (EMAG) in 1999 that central government began to give a lead. The EMAG statistics have many gaps and disadvantages, as noted earlier in this book (pages 8-13), but certainly they are a significant step forward. It will be important, in future years, for the DfEE to draw on the best practice in this field which has already been developed in certain schools and LEAs.

Principles and pitfalls

This chapter considers and discusses the principal issues and topics which formal guidance from the DfEE should in due course contain. First (Box 48), there are notes on general principles, and on specific pitfalls to avoid. The points in Box 48 are all entirely obvious and it ought to be unnecessary for a book such as this to include them. But in view of the longstanding inertia noted by Ofsted and cited above – an inertia to which Ofsted itself has frequently contributed, it must be remembered – they seem definitely worth stressing. Many of them were mentioned or implied in the earlier discussion of EMAG statistics (pages 8-13).

School profiles

Monitoring by ethnicity has two aspects. First, it is important that every school should have an up-to-date profile of its pupils by ethnicity, gender and year group. Second, there should be monitoring of various outcomes, in particular attainment in SATs and public examinations. This second type of monitoring should always be by gender as well as by ethnicity, for otherwise any major differences between the results of girls and boys will be missed and a false picture will be presented. Box 49 is an aide-memoire recalling the principal categories which may need to be used.

The categories which a school uses for describing ethnicity need to be consistent with the requirements of the DfEE in relation to the Ethnic Minority Achievement Grant, and consistent also with LEA requirements. It is neither necessary nor desirable, however, that schools should limit themselves to using the categories determined by others.

Obviously there is much more to ethnic identity than can be captured by the terms listed in Box 49. This point was stressed at length in Chapter 2 of this book: every pupil has his or her own unique mix of loyalties and belongings, and every pupil is continually developing, choosing and changing. But some information is better than no information – particularly when a school is determined to identify and deal with possible patterns and processes of discrimination and inequality.

Box 48

Monitoring by ethnicity: principles and pitfalls

1 A note on terminology

The term 'ethnic monitoring' is frequently used. The term 'ethnically-based statistics' is conceptually clearer and more accurate. So is the term used here, 'monitoring by ethnicity'.

2 The purpose of monitoring: information for decision-makers

The overall purpose of monitoring by ethnicity is to collect and collate the information which policy-makers and decision-makers need – at a range of different levels (national, LEA, school, classroom) – in order to create and maintain a more inclusive society. If a school unequivocally states that this is the purpose, and if the practical methods of collecting, analysing and publishing data clearly serve this purpose, staff and parents are likely to cooperate and assist.

3 A key distinction

It is crucial to distinguish between **monitoring of composition** ('who is here?') and the **monitoring of outcomes** ('who gets what?'). There are good reasons for doing the first on its own, so that provision can be more sensitive to need. With regard to the second, however, it is not possible to compile statistically valid data unless the first kind of monitoring takes place as well.

4 Monitoring of outcomes

The question 'who gets what?' is about both **goods** and **bads** – the benefits and resources which people want, and the penalties and disadvantages (for example, exclusion from school, or worthless paper qualifications) which they do not want. It is important that monitoring of outcomes should be concerned with both.

5 Need to know

It is helpful to distinguish between **the different levels and contexts** in which decision-makers operate. What do individual teachers need to know about the pupils in their class? A senior management team and governing body about their whole school, and how it compares with others? An LEA, both about itself and about the regional and national picture? The DfEE? Academic researchers? The concept of 'need to know' helps to clarify methods of data collection, data analysis and data sharing.

6 Categories

At present (1999) many schools and LEAs are **still not using appropriate categories**. There is still frequent use of the unhelpful category 'Black Other', and the imprecise categories 'Indian' and 'African' are used without the possibility of distinguishing between for instance, Panjabi and Gujarati or between Nigerian and Somali. Pupils from Arab, Bosnian, Turkish and Vietnamese backgrounds are among many who are simply not included. Schools and LEAs need to use more precise and appropriate categories, regardless of DfEE requirements.

9 Making comparisons in place and time

By definition, monitoring by ethnicity involves making comparisons between different ethnic groups. It should also involve making **comparisons between places** (for example, between different schools, or between different local authorities), and **comparisons over time**. Each school or LEA needs to be able to chart its progress in creating a more inclusive society, and needs to know how its own progress compares with that of others.

10 Controlling variables

It is essential to compare **like with like**. It is always relevant to check whether gender and social class are relevant variables, therefore, in addition to ethnicity. Global statements such as 'Asian pupils are performing as well as their White peers', for example, are not helpful if the groups of pupils being studied have different socio-economic profiles, or if there are significant differentials within each group between girls and boys.

11 Yardsticks for comparison

The essential yardsticks for comparison should include **national levels**, not school or LEA levels only.

12 Hard and soft data

Schools and LEAs should use not only statistical data but also **data derived from questionnaires** and focus group-type discussion. The latter should involve pupils, parents and governors as well as teachers and inspectors.

13 Leadership and support

Schools have **a right to receive guidance and practical assistance** from their LEA, and LEAs in their turn have a right to guidance and practical assistance from central government.

Box 49

Developing a school profile

The following categories should be used, unless numbers are too small to be significant. Other categories should be added, if appropriate, in any one school or local authority. Figures should be collected and shown for each year group, and separately for girls and boys. All terms refer to ethnic or cultural background, NOT nationality or citizenship status.

Black
African
> Nigerian
> Somali
> Ugandan
> Other African

Caribbean
Mixed heritage

South Asian
Bangladeshi
Indian/Gujarati
Indian/Panjabi
Pakistani
Sri Lankan
Mixed heritage
Other South Asian

White(UK and Ireland)
Irish
Travellers
English, Scottish, Welsh

Other
Albanian
Bosnian
Chinese
Kurdish
Middle East
South American
Turkish
Turkish Cypriot
Vietnamese
Other

In addition, a school needs to know how many of its pupils have arrived in UK from a non-English speaking country within the last two years, and how many belong to refugee or asylum-seeking families. Use of the term 'refugee or asylum-seeking' does not necessarily refer to legal status.

Data on attainment

There should be data by ethnicity and gender on:

- Baseline assessment
- End of Key Stage 1
- End of Key Stage 2
- End of Key Stage 3
- GCSE
- A level

At each key stage, and for each ethnic group, the data should include:

1 Number who did not reach national yardstick, most recent year. (This figure is required in connection with distribution of the Ethnic Minority Achievement Grant, between and within authorities.)

2 Percentage (as distinct from number) who did not reach national target, most recent year. (Required for making comparisons between groups.)

3 Average points score per pupil. (Required for showing profile of a whole group.)

4 Difference (+ or -) between the average points score and the national points score. (Required for seeing the school within a wider context, and for showing progress over time.)

Progress over time

A record should be kept to show progress over the years. The key figure to use, each year, is the difference (plus or minus) from the national average.

Processes and procedures

Box 51 is a questionnaire which lists key points about school-level evaluation, and which can be used to audit and review how a school is doing. It does not purport to be a scientific instrument but it is likely to be valuable as a focus for discussion and reflection in individual schools. It can be used, that is to say, to collect 'soft' or qualitative data. There are further notes on such data in the next main section of this chapter.

Qualitative approaches

The questionnaire which appears as Box 50 could not be used as a valid scientific instrument, for many of its key terms almost certainly mean different things to different people. Such a questionnaire can, however, be used to obtain a rough-and ready picture of perceptions and impressions. More especially, it can provide a trigger or focus for discussion. For example, it can be used as an agenda paper in the following contexts, amongst others:

- in a senior management team
- at a governors meeting
- at a staff meeting
- at a meeting between teachers and LEA officers or inspectors
- at a staff inset session

There are other such questionnaires elsewhere in this book, for example the one on language policy (Box 34, page 49), the one which seeks the views of pupils (Box 40, page 59), the checklist on working with parents (Box 41, page 60), and the questions to ask about an Ofsted report (Box 51, page 81). Further, the list of points to consider about curriculum subjects (pages 41-43) can readily be used as the basis for a questionnaire about staff perceptions and impressions.

Also, a good deal of other material in this book has been written and compiled in such a way as to make it appropriate and convenient for structured discussions. The practical possibilities include the following:

Box 6 (page 7), If – reflections on a life

Can be used with a simple five-point or three-point scale. In each instance the question is: 'To what extent do pupils at this school have this kind of support?'

Box 7 (page 14), The features of inclusive schools

'To what extent is this feature present at our school?' Again, a five-point scale from 'very much so' to 'not at all'.

Box 28 (page 40) Summary of objectives

Each objective can be applied to a particular lesson, module, course or programme of study.

Box 50

Analysis at school-level

To what extent is each of the following statements true at our school? With each of the items in this list, put a tick in one of the five columns on the right hand side of the page

	1 Not at all	2 A bit	3 Making progress	4 Getting there	5 Satisfactory at present
The school has information showing the current composition of each year group, by ethnicity and gender	☐	☐	☐	☐	☐
The school has information showing achievement at Key Stages 1, 2 and 3 and at GCSE and A level, as appropriate, by ethnicity and gender	☐	☐	☐	☐	☐
The school has information on baseline assessment or attainment on entry, by ethnicity and gender	☐	☐	☐	☐	☐
The school has information on pupils' experience of rewards and sanctions, by ethnicity and gender	☐	☐	☐	☐	☐
The school receives information and consultancy from the LEA, or from some other outside body, which enables it to review its own progress in comparison with similar schools elsewhere	☐	☐	☐	☐	☐
The categories for monitoring ethnicity are sufficiently detailed to be useful at school-level	☐	☐	☐	☐	☐
Other monitoring information is available and studied when appropriate, for example relating to social circumstance, entitlement to free school meals, feeder school, postcode, home language	☐	☐	☐	☐	☐
Incidents of racism and serious cultural hostility are recorded by both type and severity, and routinely reported to the local authority	☐	☐	☐	☐	☐
Good use is made of periodic surveys of staff perceptions and impressions	☐	☐	☐	☐	☐
Good use is made of surveys of parents' views and perceptions	☐	☐	☐	☐	☐
Good use is made of consultants or 'critical friends' from outside the school	☐	☐	☐	☐	☐
The principal results of monitoring are routinely reported to the school's governing body, and to the senior management team	☐	☐	☐	☐	☐
The results of monitoring are used to plan and make improvements in proviusion	☐	☐	☐	☐	☐

Box 30 (page 45) Problem-solving and thinking skills

Each item in the list can be applied to a particular lesson, module, course or programme of study.

Box 38 (page 57) Avoiding destructive conflict

Individuals can give themselves scores or marks on how well they use these skills, and on how well the staff as a whole uses them, in order to defuse conflict. They can also score or mark pupils or groups of pupils.

Box 44 (page 64) Action by schools to improve relationships

Again, each of these points can be considered on a five-point scale. The five phrases used in Box 50 would be appropriate: 'not at all', 'a bit', 'making progress', 'getting there', 'satisfactory at present'.

Evaluating the evaluators

In 1993/94, when the Ofsted system came into existence, the Runnymede Trust studied the first 50 reports to see to what extent they contained satisfactory reference to race equality issues. The title of the subsequent document issued by Runnymede, *Tales of the Uninspected*, hints at what was found – or rather, not found. In somewhat more detail:

- Only six per cent of the reports referred to race and culture issues in their 'Main Findings'.

- Only fifty per cent referred to cultural diversity issues in their reviews of what schools should do to promote pupils' cultural development.

- Less than ten per cent indicated that pupils' moral and social development might or should include learning about justice, fairness and equality.

- Not a single report indicated or implied that moral and social issues should be seen in international or global contexts.

- In references to pupil intakes and local communities, only one report referred to African-Caribbean pupils.

- Apart from a reference to a language said by the inspectors to be 'Pakistani', no report mentioned a single South Asian home or community language.

- Not a single report referred to pupils' religious affiliations and involvements.

- Not a single report treated behaviour and discipline as race equality issues. It was clear that in some of the fifty schools Black pupils were being disproportionately excluded, but no report commented on, let alone discussed, this matter.

Since those first fifty reports, Ofsted inspection teams have by and large become more sensitive to, and knowledgeable about, race equality issues. The report referred to at the start of this chapter, *Raising the Attainment of Minority Ethnic Pupils*, published in March 1999, ought to make a difference. Vigilance remains necessary, however, and it is still the case that many schools have a better appreciation of race and identity issues than do most Ofsted inspectors. Schools have both the right and the duty, it follows, on this topic more than on most, to evaluate the evaluators – or, as the phrase might be, to inspect the inspectors. The questionnaire in Box 51 could be used to study and respond to an Ofsted report. It could also be shared and discussed with an Ofsted team before or during the inspection week.

This questionnaire implies that inspection and evaluation should be an equal partnership between teachers and inspectors, and should include teachers' views of, and judgements on, inspectors or consultants who come to a school from outside. There needs to be an appropriate equality in the inspection process itself, if schools are to be supported and assisted in their endeavours to create greater equality within their own spheres of responsibility.

Views and perceptions of pupils

Evaluation should take account of the views of pupils as well as of adult professionals. One of the questionnaires in this book (Box 40, page 59) is specifically about the views and feelings of pupils. There is much other material in the book which can be used as a focus or trigger for discussions with pupils and students. In particular, the following items are suitable, either exactly as they stand or modified if appropriate:

- Box 3 (page 4), 'Get out of my class!'

- Box 4 (page 5), Respect – a teenager talking

- Box 5 (page 6), Life and life-chances

- Box 10 (page 19), 'Yu af fe play like yu a bad man'

- Box 11 (page 19), All this pressure

- Box 12 (page 20), Street cred and school norms

- Box 27 (page 38), Racism in and around the school: taking action

- Box 36 (page 54), What next? – stories and situations

- Box 37 (page 56), Classroom management situations

- Box 38 (page 57), Avoiding destructive conflict

Box 51

Judging an Ofsted report

This questionnaire shows the points on which staff and governors may reasonably expect guidance and comment from an Ofsted inspection. It could be shown to inspectors before the inspection begins, together with a commentary on the school's own perceptions of its strengths and needs, and could also be a useful focus for discussion after the report has been published.

		1 NO	2	3	4	5 YES
1	The report comments accurately and helpfully on the school's policy documentation relating to equal opportunities	☐	☐	☐	☐	☐
2	The report comments accurately and helpfully on the school's use of staff appointed under the Ethnic Minority Achievement Grant	☐	☐	☐	☐	☐
3	The report comments accurately and helpfully on the school's arrangements for monitoring attainment by ethnicity and gender	☐	☐	☐	☐	☐
4	The report comments accurately and helpfully on the special training which staff have received in relation to equal opportunities issues	☐	☐	☐	☐	☐
5	The report contains helpful judgements about:					
	• Language and bilingualism	☐	☐	☐	☐	☐
	• Curriculum content	☐	☐	☐	☐	☐
	• Contacts with parents and carers	☐	☐	☐	☐	☐
	• Dealing with racist behaviour	☐	☐	☐	☐	☐
	• Gender issues	☐	☐	☐	☐	☐
	• Cultural and religious sensitivity	☐	☐	☐	☐	☐
6	The report reflects sound knowledge of equal opportunities issues	☐	☐	☐	☐	☐
7	The report comments helpfully on equal opportunities issues in relation to the literacy hour and the numeracy hour	☐	☐	☐	☐	☐

REFERENCES

This last section of the book contains background references,
lists some recent publications for further reading, and provides
addresses and telephone numbers of organisations which
provide useful information and resources.

Headings in this chapter

References

Get out of my class! (Box 3)

Cecile Wright has been an influential author for many years. She is co-author with Debbie Weeks of *Improving Practice*, Runnymede Trust 1998, and is one of the authors of a new book on exclusions published in 1999 by Falmer Press. (See bibliography below for fuller details.) She is currently reader in sociology at Nottingham Trent University.

The features of inclusive schools (Box 7)

The book *Making the Difference* by Maud Blair and Jill Bourne and their co-authors is well worth obtaining and consulting. It is based on visits to 28 schools which had been especially recommended by Ofsted as centres of good practice. There are also some quotations from the book in Box 35. It was commissioned from the Open University by the DfEE.

Components of an inclusive society (Box 8)

The ideas summarised here are illustrated at length in *Cities Against Racism*, a report on a European Commission project published in 1999 by Greenwich Council. Full details and a summary are available from Social Inclusion and Justice Unit, 27 Wellington Street, Woolwich, London SW17 7PW.

Identity and teenage racism (Box 15)

Publications from Greenwich over the years include *Sagaland*, a resource for better understanding white youth sub-cultures; *Routes of Racism* by Roger Hewitt, together with a training video and handbook for youth leaders; and *Race Tracks* by Sheila Dadzie. Full details from the Greenwich Social Inclusion and Justice Unit, address above.

'Stand up if you're proud...' (Page 16)

The play *Ooh Ah Showab Khan* by Clifford Oliver was developed by the Arc Theatre Ensemble with financial support from the European Commission and the London Borough of Barking and Dagenham.

Self and other (Box 19)

The book *Equality Assurance in Schools* was developed by the Runnymede Trust to show how racial justice and cultural diversity issues can be incorporated into all subjects in the national curriculum. It was first published in 1993 and has frequently been reprinted. It is quoted also in Boxes 28 and 33.

Planning an anti-racist course (Box 29)

This is quoted from a paper entitled 'Why is History always White?' by Teresa Clark, deputy head of Lilian Baylis School, Lambeth.

The features of curriculum English (Box 30)

The book *Enriching Literacy: talk, texts and tales in today's classroom* is based on courses and projects organised by Brent Language Service in the period 1996-98. It draws extensively on theories developed by Professor Jim Cummins in Canada. See also other books on bilingualism mentioned on page 85, particularly the titles by Josie Levine and Norah McWilliam.

Reviewing language policy (Box 34)

This questionnaire is derived from material prepared by the Insted consultancy for Slough Borough Council, 1999. It draws also on consultancy work by Insted with Brent and Hounslow.

Successful relationships (Box 35)

See also the note on Box 7. The school in Box 35 is referred to in *Making the Difference* as 'Northern Catholic High School'.

Avoiding destructive conflict (Box 38)

This list incorporates several points in Tony Sewell's book *Black Masculinities*, based on extensive case-study research in one secondary school. Sewell's interest is particularly in how teachers can avoid provoking and escalating needless confrontations with Black students. See also on this subject David Gillborn's *Racism and Antiracism in Real Schools*. There are details of both books in the list on page 85.

Reducing exclusions (Box 42)

The project referred to here (and also in Box 43) was funded under Section 11 arrangements. It was initiated by the LEA, in close partnership with the school, in the light of extensive monitoring. The descriptions here are compiled from papers submitted by the LEA for the creation of this book.

Action by schools (Box 44)

There is a useful and up-to-date summary of key issues by Audrey Osler and John Hill in 'Exclusion from school and racial equality: an examination of government proposals in the light of recent research evidence', *Cambridge Journal of Education*, Vol 29 No 1, 1999. The government's proposals are outlined in *Truancy and School Exclusion*, published by the Social Exclusion Unit in 1998. Audrey Osler, now professor of education at the University of Leicester, is also the author of *Exclusion from School and Racial Equality: research report*, published by the Commission for Racial Equality in 1997. Acknowledgement is due also to the Working Group on Racism in Children's Resources (address on page 86) and to ideas in *Improving Practice* by Debbie Weekes and Cecile Wright. *The Pupil Exclusion Maze* by Paul Boyd contains useful information: details from QEC Publications, PO Box 3368, London N20 0UQ.

Secondments for whole-school change (Box 46)

This is a fictitious project. The original paper describing it was prepared by Robin Richardson for a conference on language teaching, particularly with regard to new approaches in the use of Section 11 resources, organised by the School Curriculum and Assessment Authority (SCAA) in 1995.

African-Caribbean Achievement Project (Box 47)

A version of this paper was provided by the Insted consultancy for a real school, as a basis for real planning in relation to the Ethnic Minority Achievement Grant, 1999. Fuller information is available from Insted, address on page 86.

Monitoring by ethnicity (Box 49)

This is a shortened version of a memorandum submitted by the Insted consultancy to the Department for Education and Employment, in response to the White Paper *Excellence in Schools*, 1996.

Useful books

General

Blair, Maud and Bourne, Jill *et al* (1998) **Making the Difference: teaching and learning strategies in successful multi-ethnic schools**, Department for Education and Employment.

Gillborn, David (1995) **Racism and Antiracism in Real Schools**, Open University Press.

Gillborn, David and Gipps, Caroline (1996), **Recent Research on the Achievements of Minority Ethnic Pupils**, The Stationery Office.

Klein, Gillian (1995) **Education towards Race Equality**, Cassell.

May, Stephen, *ed* (1999) **Critical Multiculturalism, rethinking multicultural and antiracist education**, Open University Press.

Nieto, Sonia (1999) **The Light in their Eyes: creating multicultural learning communities**, Teachers College Press and Trentham Books.

Office for Standards in Education (1999) **Raising the Attainment of Minority Ethnic Pupils**, Office of Her Majesty's Chief Inspector of Schools.

Runnymede Trust (1993) **Equality Assurance in Schools: quality, identity, society**, Runnymede Trust with Trentham.

Wright, Cecile (1992) **Race Relations in the Primary School**, David Fulton.

Wright, Cecile *et al* (1999) **'Race', Class and Gender in Exclusion from School**, Falmer Press.

Early Years

Brown, Babette (1998) **Unlearning Discrimination in the Early Years**, Trentham.

Early Years Anti Racist Training Network (1998) **Planning for Excellence: implementing the DfEE guidance requirement for the equal opportunity strategy in early years development plans**, available from EYTARN, P O Box 28, Wallasey L45 9LA.

Siraj-Blatchford, Iram (1994) **The Early Years: laying the foundations for racial equality**, Trentham.

The Educational Experience of African-Caribbean pupils

Chambers, Christine *et al* (1996) **Celebrating Identity: a resource manual**, Trentham.

Channer, Yvonne (1995) **I Am a Promise: the school achievement of British African-Caribbeans**, Trentham.

de la Mothe, Gordon (1993) **Reconstructing the Black Image**, Trentham.

Nehaul, Kamala (1996) **The Schooling of Children of Caribbean Heritage**, Trentham.

Runnymede Trust (1996) **This is where I Live: stories and pressures in Brixton**, Runnymede Trust.

Sewell, Tony (1997) **Black Masculinities and Schooling: how Black boys survive modern schooling**, Trentham.

Weekes, Debbie and Wright, Cecile (1998) **Improving Practice: a whole school approach to raising the achievement of African Caribbean youth**, Runnymede Trust.

Culture and Religion

Jackson, Robert and Nesbitt, Eleanor (1993) **Hindu Children in Britain**, Trentham.

Parker-Jenkins. Marie (1995) **Children of Islam: a teacher's guide to meeting the needs of Muslim pupils**, Trentham.

Runnymede Trust (1997) **Islamophobia: a challenge for us all**, Runnymede Trust.

Language and Bilingualism

Alladina, Safder (1995) **Being Bilingual: a guide for parents, teachers and young people**, Trentham.

Brent Language Service (1999) **Enriching Literacy: text, talk and tales in today's classroom**, Trentham.

Cummins, Jim (1997) **Negotiating Identities: education for empowerment in a diverse society**, CABE, distributed by Trentham.

Drever, Mina, Moule, Susan and Keith Peterson (1999) **Teaching English in Primary Classrooms**, Trentham.

Edwards, Viv (1998) **The Power of Babel: teaching and learning in multilingual classrooms**, Trentham.

Gibbons, Pauline(1991) **Learning to Learn in a Second Language**, Primary English Teaching Association, Australia.

Gravelle, Maggie (1996) **Supporting Bilingual Learners in Schools**, Trentham.

Language and Curriculum Access Service (1995) **Making Progress: teaching and assessment in the multilingual classroom**, London Borough of Enfield.

Language and Curriculum Access Service (1997) **Scaffolding learning in the multilingual classroom**, London Borough of Enfield.

Levine, Josie (1996) **Developing Pedagogies in the Multilingual Classroom**, Trentham.

McWilliam, Norah (1998) **What's in a Word? – vocabulary development in multilingual classrooms**, Trentham.

In addition, there are useful resource lists available from Centre for Language in Primary Education, Intercultural Education Partnership, Mantra Publishing, National Association for Language Development in the Currriculum, Partnership Publishing and Tamarind Books. Addresses on page 86.

Refugee and asylum seeking pupils

Abebaw, Meron *et al* (1998) **Let's Spell It Out: peer research on the educational support needs of young refugees and asylum seekers**, Save the Children.

Kahin, Mohamed (1997) **Educating Somali Children in Britain**, Trentham.

Rutter, Jill and Hyder, Tina (1994) **Refugee Children in the Classroom**, Trentham with Save the Children.

Jones, Crispin and Rutter, Jill (1998) **Refugee Education: mapping the field**, Trentham.

Richman, Naomi (1998) **In the Midst of the Whirlwind: a manual for helping refugee children**, Trentham.

In addition: many valuable materials are produced by the Refugee Council, 3 Bondway, London SW8 1SJ. Tel 0171 582 6922.

Useful addresses and contacts

Association of London Government, 36 Old Queen Street, London SW1H 9JF. Tel 0171 447 6211.

Brent Language Service, Centre for Staff Development, Brentfield Road, London NW10 8HE. Tel 0181 937 3370.

Centre for Language in Primary Education, Webber Row, London SE1 8QW. Tel 0171 633 0840.

Commission for Racial Equality, 10/12 Allington Street, London SW1 5EH. Tel 0171 828 7022.

Development Education Centre, Selly Oak Colleges, Bristol Road, Birmingham B29 6LE. Tel: 0121 472 3255.

Early Years Training Anti Racist Network, PO Box 28, Wallasey L45 9LA.

Insted, The Old School, Kilburn Park Road, London NW6 5XA. Tel 0171 372 0965.

Institute of Race Relations, 2-6 Leeke Street, King's Cross Road, London WC1X 9HS. Tel 0171 833 2010.

Intercultural Education Partnership, 17 Barford Street, Islington, London N1 0QB. Tel 0171 226 8885.

Mantra Publishing, 5 Alexandra Grove, London N12 8NU. Tel 0181 445 5123.

Mediation UK, Alexander House, Telephone Avenue, Bristol BS1 4BS. Tel: 0117 904 6661.

Multilingual Matters, Frankfurt Lodge, Clevedon Hall, Victoria Road, Clevedon, Somerset BS21 7SJ.

National Association for Language Development in the Curriculum (NALDIC), South West Herts LCSC, Holywell School Site, Tolpits Lane, Watford WD1 8NT. Tel 0192 322 5130.

1990 Trust, Southbank Technopark, 90 London Road, London SE1 6LN. Tel 0171 717 1579.

Partnership Publishing, Department of Teaching Studies, Bradford and Ilkley Community College, Great Horton Road, Bradford BD7 1AY. Tel 0127 475 3464.

Race On The Agenda, 356 Holloway Road, London N7 6PA. Tel: 0171 700 8135.

Reading and Language Information Centre, University of Reading, Bulmershe Court, Earley, Reading RG6 1HY. Tel 0118 931 8820.

Refugee Council, 3 Bondway, London SW8 1SJ. Tel 0171 582 6922.

Resource Centre for Multicultural Education, Forest Lodge Education Centre, Charnor Road, Leicester LE3 6LH. Tel 0116 231 3399.

Runnymede Trust, 133 Aldersgate Street, London EC1A 4JA. Tel 0171 600 9666.

Save the Children, Cambridge House, Cambridge Grove, London W6 0LE. Tel 0181 741 4054.

Tamarind Books, Box 296, Camberley, Surrey GU15 4WD. Tel 0127 668 3979.

The Place To Be, Edinburgh House, 154-182 Kennington Lane, London SE11 4EZ. Tel 0171 820 6487.

Trentham Books, Westview House, 734 London Road, Oakhill, Stoke-on-Trent, Staffordshire ST4 5NP. Tel 01782 745567.

Working Group on Racism in Children's Resources, 46 Wandsworth Road, London SW8 3LX. Tel: 0171 627 4594.

Websites

For all issues relating to racial justice in Britain, it is valuable to visit the website of the 1990 Trust: *http://www.blink.org.uk* It contains links to many other organisations, including several throughout Europe as well as in the UK.

On teaching English as an additional language, it is valuable to join the mailing list of *mailto:eal-bilingual@ngfl.gov.uk*

Save the Children is at *http://www.savethechildren.org.uk*

The Insted consultancy is at *http://www.insted.co.uk*

The full Trentham Books catalogue is at *http://www.trentham-books.co.uk*

Keeping up-to-date

For up-to-date information on newly published resources, consult the journal *Multicultural Teaching*, ISSN 0263 0869. Details from Trentham Books, address above.